# I Can Problem Solve®

INTERMEDIATE
ELEMENTARY
GRADES

SECOND EDITION

## An Interpersonal Cognitive Problem-Solving Program

**Myrna B. Shure**

I Can Problem Solve® is a registered trademark of Myrna B. Shure.

Research Press   2612 North Mattis Avenue   Champaign, Illinois 61822   (800) 519-2707   www.researchpress.com

Illustrations by Herbert Wimble
Cover design and illustration by Doug Burnett
Composition by Wadley Graphix Corporation
Printed by Malloy Lithographing


ISBN 0–87822–471–8
Library of Congress Catalog No. 2001087210

This book is dedicated to Robin Joselit Weigert,
a consummate problem solver who, at age 10,
brought some games to life by brilliantly (and patiently)
playing them out when they were first conceived
and put to paper—and who created the sample
continuation story told in Lesson 17.

It is also dedicated to our spirited troupe of critics,
ages 10 and 11, whose own ideas sparked
constant change as we took the program to the schools.

# CONTENTS

# PROBLEM-SOLVING SKILLS

# LIST OF COMPLEMENTARY APPLICATIONS

# ACKNOWLEDGMENTS

The research phase for developing this program was funded by grants #R01-27741 (1977-1979) and #R01-MH35989 (1981-1985), awarded to Myrna B. Shure and George Spivack by the National Institute of Mental Health, Washington, DC. To Dr. Constance E. Clayton, Superintendent, and Leontine D. Scott, Associate Superintendent of School Operations, School District of Philadelphia, deep appreciation is expressed for their support of ICPS in the schools throughout the years. Thanks also for the collaboration of Dr. Irvin J. Farber, Director of Research for the School District of Philadelphia during the research phase.

Special thanks go to George Spivack, whose initial research with adolescents demonstrated a clear association between interpersonal cognitive problem-solving skills and behavior. His vision—that enhancing interpersonal thinking skills could reduce or prevent high-risk behaviors—inspired the creation of day-by-day lesson-games to reach those goals. George's help and guidance were instrumental in identifying age-appropriate skills and paved the way for the present program for the intermediate elementary grades.

A very special thank you to everyone at Research Press, particularly to Ann Wendel, President, Russell Pence, Vice President of Marketing, and Dennis Wiziecki, Advertising Manager, for their belief in and enthusiasm for ICPS programming in the schools; to Suzanne Wagner, for her design of the pages, which makes them pleasing to look at and easy to read; and to my editor, Karen Steiner, who in her own inimitable style of ICPS let me know that "There's more than one way" to express a thought. Karen's careful attention to the littlest details and her patience with my never-ending questions made me feel safe and secure.

Special recognition goes to our participating research teachers, who not only conducted the program with their fifth- and sixth-grade classes, but also helped to improve techniques for presenting the lessons to children and provided many of the informal problem-solving dialogues. To these Philadelphia teachers and to their principals, whose continued cooperation and enthusiastic support made this program possible, we are deeply grateful:

*Blaine Elementary School:* Madeline Cartwright, principal, Christine Mathis, teacher

*Hanna Elementary School:* Dr. James Clements, principal, Joyce Hendricks, Mary Lucus, and Anne O'Neil, teachers

*Leidy Elementary School:* Bernard Belasco, principal, Arletha Allen, teacher

*Locke Elementary School:* Dr. James Barksdale, principal, Rita Exconde and Cynthia Williams, teachers

*Meade Elementary School:* Mark Levin, principal, Penny Myers, Alberta Robinson, Anita Schumer, June Siegel, and Lynnette Stewart, teachers

*Pratt Elementary School:* Dr. Thomas Young, principal, Genvieve Boulden, Nathaniel Coe, Rosalie Funderbuck, and Leonard Thompson, teachers

*T. M. Peirce Elementary School:* Albert Cohen, principal, Sherry Hopkins, Elnora Marcus, and Kerry Weiner, teachers

Thanks also go to William Snyder, who, in becoming principal of the Leidy School upon Bernard Belasco's retirement, became an important addition to our team, as did Carol Mullen, who became principal of T. M. Peirce, and Janet Samuels, who became principal at Locke during ongoing ICPS research at those schools.

Gratitude is expressed to Gladys Holzbaur, a teacher at St. Leo's Elementary School; to our research assistants, Linda Deuschle and Cheryl Standen, for their creative contributions during program development; to Cheryl Standen, for the stick-figure drawings created for the problem-solving section of the program; and to William Renn for Illustrations 6, 13, and 14.

We also thank participating research teachers Arletha Allen, Sherry Hopkins, Penny Myers, and June Siegel for their additional consultation upon completion of the program, which led to further revisions incorporated into this volume. But it was our greatest critics of all, in grades five and six, who helped us shape these lessons into their final form. A very special tribute to them.

# INTRODUCTION

Every day, some kind of interpersonal problem comes up between children, a child and a teacher, or a child and other figures in authority. Some children can cope with and solve these kinds of problems very well; others are considerably less able or willing to think them through. Still, all children can benefit from systematic practice and application of problem-solving skills when typical difficulties between people come up in the course of daily living.

This volume, along with two companion volumes designed for preschool and kindergarten/primary grades, shows teachers how to help children learn to solve the problems they have with others.* The approach employed, originally called Interpersonal Cognitive Problem Solving, has come to be called ICPS by the many adults and children who have used it. Although children with serious emotional disturbances will likely require more individual attention and/or outside professional help, ICPS offers a practical approach to help most children learn to evaluate and deal with problems. Its underlying goal is to help children learn *how* to think, not *what* to think. It does not tell them what to do when conflict or other problem situations come up. Rather, it gives children ways to talk about their view of problems and think problems through. The main goal, focus, content, method, and benefits of ICPS are summarized on the following page.

As this summary suggests, the benefits of ICPS training are numerous. Based on studies of thousands of children and their teachers conducted over a period of 20 years, we have learned that, as early as age 4, youngsters who learn how to use ICPS skills in time become less impatient, over-emotional, and aggressive, as well as better liked and more concerned about their peers in distress. Overly inhibited youngsters become more outgoing, better able to express their feelings, and more likely to enter into activities with others. Given these findings and the fact that problems and emotional difficulties peak between the fourth and fifth grades, a program for this age group is especially important.

What can you expect from children as the program progresses? Teachers report that, within the first few weeks, most children begin to adopt ICPS concepts outside of formal training, especially words describing people's feelings.

In this age group, it appears that behaviors relating to positive peer sociability, including concern for others and for being liked by peers, are the first to change. These gains can be seen shortly after the lessons

---

The other volumes in the program, *I Can Problem Solve: An Interpersonal Cognitive Problem-Solving Program (Preschool)* and *I Can Problem Solve: An Interpersonal Cognitive Problem-Solving Program (Kindergarten and Primary Grades)*, are also available from Research Press. For information about immediate and long-term scientific research findings, as well as about measures of alternative solution skills and consequential thinking skills, contact Dr. Myrna Shure, Drexel University, 245 N. 15th St., MS–626, Philadelphia, PA 19102.

# THE ICPS PROGRAM

**GOAL**      To teach children thinking skills that can be used to help resolve or prevent "people" problems

**FOCUS**      Teaches children *how* to think, not *what* to think
Guides children to think for themselves
Teaches children how to evaluate their own ideas
Encourages children to come up with many solutions to problems on their own

**CONTENT**      **Pre-Problem-Solving Skills**
Learning a problem-solving vocabulary
Identifying one's own and others' feelings
Considering other people's points of view
Learning sequencing and timing of events

                        **Problem-Solving Skills**
Thinking of more than one solution
Considering consequences
Deciding which solution to choose
Thinking of a sequenced, step-by-step plan to reach a goal

**METHOD**      Teaches skills through the use of games, stories, puppets, and role-playing
Guides the use of skills in real-life situations
Integrates ideas into standard curriculum

**BENEFITS**      **For Children**
Fun for children—presents lessons in game form
Builds self-confidence
Builds listening skills
Encourages generation of alternative solutions
Provides skills to handle new problems
Facilitates social interaction among peers
Teaches skills applicable to other situations
Increases sensitivity to others, sharing, and caring
Increases independence
Increases ability to wait
Increases ability to cope with frustration
Decreases impulsivity
Decreases social withdrawal

                        **For Teachers**
Reinforces other curriculum goals
Creates a more positive classroom atmosphere
Decreases time spent handling conflicts
Enhances teachers' own problem-solving skills
Deepens insight into children's thoughts and feelings

devoted to pre-problem-solving skills are completed and the lessons on problem-solving skills are begun. Impulsive and inhibited behaviors take longer to change in this age group than in younger children, perhaps because these behaviors are more habituated. However, by program's end, children who still behave impulsively or are still overly inhibited are more able to think about what they do or do not do in ways that suggest behavior change may soon follow. Our research with children exposed to this curriculum in fifth and sixth grades has supported this possibility. By the end of sixth grade, impulsive and inhibited behaviors were well below those of youngsters not exposed to ICPS training.

Research also shows that gains in ICPS skills have an important indirect impact on academic achievement. Within a wide range of IQ (80–120+), gains in ICPS are linked with improvements in interpersonal behaviors, which are in turn linked with gains in objectively measured math and reading levels. It appears that once behaviors mediated through ICPS skills improve, youngsters can better absorb the task-oriented demands of the classroom and subsequently do better in school.

Although it does take time for major behavior changes to occur, children enjoy the ICPS program, and teachers find it rewarding when children learn to think for themselves.

## PROGRAM OVERVIEW

The ICPS program for intermediate elementary grades includes both formal lessons and specific suggestions for incorporating ICPS principles in classroom interactions and the curriculum.

### ICPS Lesson Content

Each of the 77 ICPS lessons contains a stated purpose or purposes, list of suggested materials, and a teacher script. The teacher script, intended as a flexible guideline, explains the basic steps in conducting the lesson.

As the outline on the following page shows, the lessons are grouped into two major categories: pre-problem-solving skills and problem-solving skills. The ICPS words and other pre-problem-solving concepts set the stage for the problem-solving skills, which are associated with alternative solutions, consequences, solution-consequence pairs, and means-ends thinking.

Throughout the entire program, the concept "There's more than one way" is stressed to help children develop a problem-solving style of thought. There's more than one way to:

- Explain another's behavior (for example, "Maybe he didn't wave because he's angry with me" or "Maybe he just didn't see me")
- Explain another's motivation (for example, "Maybe that girl sitting by herself wants to be alone" or "Maybe the others won't let her play")
- Find out others' feelings and preferences (by watching, listening, and asking)
- Solve a problem (with different solutions and step-by-step plans)

# OUTLINE OF ICPS LESSONS

| LESSONS | PURPOSE |
|---|---|
| | **Pre-Problem-Solving Skills** |
| 1–2 | To help children begin to develop sensitivity toward and awareness of others |
| | To focus on ICPS concepts relating to negation (IS-NOT) and choices (OR-AND) |
| 3 | To help children realize that there are some things people cannot do at the SAME TIME |
| 4–6 | To foster sensitivity to people's feelings by reviewing familiar feeling words: HAPPY, ANGRY, SAD, AFRAID, and JEALOUS |
| | To suggest that not everyone feels the same way about the same thing |
| 7–9 | To help children recognize the importance of listening to others, of getting the whole message, and of getting information directly from the original source |
| 10–11 | To expand children's repertoire of feeling words to include FRUSTRATED, IMPATIENT, LONELY, SYMPATHETIC, ASHAMED, EMBARRASSED, and SURPRISED |
| 12–13 | To give children practice in paying attention and remembering, a precursor to sensitivity to others' feelings, needs, and preferences |
| 14–19 | To highlight the feeling words DISAPPOINTED, PROUD, WORRIED, and RELIEVED |
| | To promote further thought about one's own and others' feelings, including the impact of one's behavior |
| 20–21 | To introduce the concept "There's more than one way" of thinking by focusing on different ways of observing: listening, watching, and asking |
| 22–24 | As a precursor to consequential thinking, to encourage further consideration of how and why two people can have different perspectives and feelings |

Children are also helped to see that there's more than one potential consequence should a solution or plan be carried out. ICPS teachers never tell children solutions, consequences, or steps in a means-ends plan. Rather, they encourage children to think of their own ideas and then to evaluate, in light of potential consequences, whether those ideas are or are not good ones.

## Conducting ICPS Lessons

Teachers have found the following suggestions for conducting ICPS lessons helpful with children in the intermediate elementary grades:

1. Refer to the lessons as games, when appropriate, to create a positive atmosphere for learning. Or you can just begin the lesson by saying, "Today's ICPS activity is . . ." or "We're going to do ICPS now." Let the children call the program ICPS, which to them can mean I Can Problem Solve.

2. Begin the program as early as possible in the school year. You can then introduce lessons at a leisurely pace and avoid surprising children with a sudden shift in the way you handle problem situations. Some teachers have integrated ICPS into their lesson plans for one 40- to 45-minute period three times a week. If the program is started early on, conducting ICPS lessons three times a week will be sufficient to complete the entire series well within the school year.

3. Proceed at the pace appropriate to the abilities and interests of your class. If your class shows a lack of interest in some of the early pre-problem-solving lessons, you can move through them more quickly. Do not skip these early lessons entirely, however—they form the basis for the more sophisticated later lessons. If your class is having problems grasping a particular concept, this need not be a stumbling block. Ample repetition of main concepts exists in the lessons, and most children will eventually catch on.

4. Some lessons are designed for the participation of a specific leader or group of actors or players. Explain to children not chosen for these roles that there will be plenty of other opportunities to participate during the course of the program.

5. Feel free to adapt the wording or content of any lesson, as long as the concepts to be taught are not lost. It is not necessary to memorize the teacher script. At first, you may wish to place the script on your desk or lap and casually read from it. Once you are comfortable with the style of eliciting responses, you may be able to get along without the script at all.

6. Most of the lessons can be conducted with the entire class. In lessons where small groups form, try to mix children who respond freely and those who are less responsive. Because ICPS involves a great deal of interaction, an entire group composed of the latter could result in group silence. As much as possible, try to place particularly disruptive children who are friends in separate groups.

7. Teachers have found that enthusiasm for ICPS does not diminish when, within limits, some of the activities are assigned as homework. Homework and the option of having children write their responses may be beneficial if you use some kind of feedback (for example, reading aloud, having children pair off and compare ideas, written notes from you). It is important not to overuse the homework option, however.

8. Be sure to apply the ICPS concepts taught in the lessons informally, in classroom interactions, as well as to build the concepts into the curriculum. Doing so gives children the opportunity to practice their newly acquired thinking skills. These applications should continue after the formal lessons are completed.

9. If desired, create an in-school newsletter and include child-reported episodes of successful problem solving. Another option is to appoint, or let the class appoint, an "ICPS Kid of the Day." Let this child announce over the school public address system how he or she solved a problem, read an ICPS-created story, and so forth.

## Complementary Applications

Having children associate how they think with what they do in real-life situations is essential to the success of the program. As noted previously, suggestions are made periodically throughout the book for applying ICPS skills in the classroom—both in interpersonal situations that may arise during the day and in the curriculum. Suggestions for interaction in the classroom and integration in the curriculum are given after the lesson or group of lessons to which they pertain. Presented on bordered pages, these complementary applications are just as important as the formal lessons.

## Illustrations, Activity Sheets, and Mini-Plays

The ICPS lessons make use of illustrations, activity sheets, and mini-plays, which immediately follow the lessons to which they pertain. All of these materials may be copied for classroom use. You may wish to enlarge the illustrations so children can see and point to them easily during the lesson, or you may place the illustrations under an opaque projector.

Other suggested materials are readily available in the classroom: chalkboard or easel, paper and pencils, art supplies, and the like. Substitutes for hand puppets, suggested in some lessons, may include paper bags, socks, or children's reading the parts of the puppets. Children this age also enjoy making their own puppets.

## Appendix Content

Two appendixes complete this volume. Appendix A offers some guidelines for continued ICPS teaching once the formal lessons have been completed. Some questions are included to help teachers think about how they can communicate key ICPS concepts to children. This appendix also includes the ICPS Teacher Self-Evaluation Checklist, intended to help teachers gauge their ability to use ICPS teaching on an ongoing basis.

Appendix B offers a summary of the steps and questions teachers ask in dialoguing child-child and teacher-child problems. These pages can be duplicated and posted in the classroom to help teachers remember how to use the ICPS approach when everyday problems arise.

## ICPS DIALOGUING

Central to the ICPS program is the process of problem-solving dialoguing. In ICPS dialoguing, the teacher guides the child in applying ICPS concepts to solve a real-life problem. This type of dialoguing reflects a style of thought that will help children try again if their first attempt to solve a problem should fail and learn to cope with frustration when their desires must be delayed or denied.

The program contains many examples of dialoguing. Even very early in the program, the teacher may conduct what are called "mini-dialogues" with children. After Lessons 1 through 48 have been completed, the children will be ready for full ICPS dialogues in which they identify a problem, generate alternative solutions, and choose the best solution. After Lesson 67, you may wish to conduct means-ends dialogues, or dialogues in which you elicit a step-by-step plan for dealing with a problem situation.

## ICPS Dialoguing Procedures

The nature of the problem that arises will determine the exact procedures for ICPS dialoguing. You will not need to memorize a set of specific steps or questions. However, the steps and questions next presented will give you a sense of what is involved in dialoguing child-child problems and in resolving teacher-child conflicts.

In general, you will want to help children identify the problem, appreciate their own and others' feelings, think of solutions to the problem, and anticipate the consequences of a solution (see Steps 1–6). If appropriate, you may want to encourage means-ends thinking, or thinking about potential obstacles, sequences of events, and time or timing (see Steps 7–9). Praising the thinking process (Step 10) is also important.

### Child-child problems

STEP 1: Define the problem.

What happened? What's the matter?

That will help me understand the problem better.

STEP 2: Elicit feelings.

How do you feel?

How does _____ feel?

STEP 3: Elicit consequences.

What happened when you did that?

STEP 4: Elicit feelings about consequences.

How did you feel when _____?
(*For example:* He took your pencil/she hit you)

STEP 5: Encourage the child to think of alternative solutions.

Can you think of a DIFFERENT way to solve this problem so _____?
(*For example:* You both won't be mad/she won't hit you)

STEP 6: Encourage evaluation of the solution.

Is that a good idea or not a good idea?

*If a good idea:* Go ahead and try that.

*If not a good idea:* Oh, you'll have to think of something DIFFERENT.

STEP 7: Encourage the child to think of potential obstacles.

Could anything stop you from doing that?

STEP 8: Encourage sequential thinking.

What is the next thing you could say or do?

STEP 9: Guide thought about time or timing.

How long might that take?

Is this a GOOD TIME to do that?

STEP 10: Praise the child's act of thinking.

You're thinking this through very well.

## Teacher-child problems

Can I talk to you and to _____ at the SAME TIME?

Is that a GOOD PLACE to _____?
(*For example:* Draw/leave your food)

Can you think of a GOOD PLACE to _____?

Is this a GOOD TIME to _____?
(*For example:* Talk to your neighbor/talk to me)

When is a GOOD TIME?

How do you think I feel when you _____?
(*For example:* Don't listen/throw food/interrupt me)

Can you think of something DIFFERENT to do until _____?
(*For example:* I can get what you want/I can help you)

Once children become accustomed to ICPS dialoguing, most can respond to a considerably shortened version of questioning. For instance, just asking, "Can you think of a DIFFERENT idea?" is often enough to cue children that they need to apply their problem-solving skills.

## Basic Principles of ICPS Dialoguing

Five basic principles, applicable to children as young as age 4, underlie the dialoguing process. The only prerequisite is that children understand the basic word concepts used by the adult. Relatively consistent application of these principles in time helps children associate their newly acquired thinking skills with what they do and how they behave.

*First, both child and teacher must identify the problem.* Casually saying, "What happened?"; "What's the matter?"; or "Tell me about it" not only helps the child clarify the problem but also ensures that you will not jump to a faulty conclusion about what is going on. For example: "Oh, now I see what the *problem* is. I thought you were mad because your friend took your book. Now I see it's because she had it too long and won't give it back." Discovering the child's view of the problem starts the dialoguing process on the proper course.

*Second, when dialoguing, it is important to understand and deal with the real problem.* The child in the preceding example thinks he has already shared his book with his friend, but the teacher may see this child grab the book and erroneously assume that grabbing is the problem. Actually, grabbing is the child's *solution* to the problem of getting his book back, not the problem itself. From the child's point of view, the real problem is that he wants his book back.

*Third, once the real problem has been identified, the teacher must not alter it to fit his or her own needs.* Suppose that the teacher becomes intent on showing the child in the example how to share his things. Because the child is thinking only about how to get back something he knows he has already shared, the teacher's guidance will likely lead to resistance. In this case, attempting to teach the "right" thing may backfire.

*Fourth, the child, not the teacher, must solve the problem.* If the child is to develop the habit of thinking of his own solutions to problems and considering the potential consequences of his actions, he must be encouraged to think for himself. More than simply "listening" to the child, the teacher must actively draw out what the child thinks caused the problem, how he and others feel about the situation, his ideas about how to solve the difficulty, and what he thinks might happen if he were to put those ideas into action. In highlighting the child's thinking, the teacher does not offer solutions to the problem or suggest what might happen next. When not bombarded with "don'ts" or offered a stream of suggestions about "do's," the child is freed to think through the problem and decide for himself what and what not to do. The teacher only asks questions and, through these, guides and encourages the emergence of problem-solving thinking.

*Finally, the focus is on* how *the child thinks, not on* what *he thinks (in other words, the specific conclusions he comes to).* Research on the ICPS program suggests that the process of a child's thinking is more important in the long run than the content of a specific solution. Attention is therefore focused on developing a style of thinking that will help the child deal with interpersonal problems in general, not on solving the immediate problem to the teacher's satisfaction (although this often occurs). Praising a solution may inhibit further thought about other ideas. Criticizing a solution may inhibit the child's speaking freely about what is on his mind. In either case, the child's thinking will shift from generating options, consequences, and causes to selecting the one thing that meets with teacher approval. In applying these principles, the teacher transmits to the child the value judgment that *thinking* is important, and the child learns that thinking meets with adult approval.

## When Not to Dialogue

It is not possible or even necessary to dialogue every problem that comes up. In fact, there are times when dialoguing is not effective and its use is better postponed. Clearly, if a child has been or is likely to be physically harmed, your first priority is to help by removing the child from danger.

In addition, sometimes a crying child just needs to cry—an angry child just needs to be angry. For example, Roberta, a super problem solver and socially competent child, was fighting with Vanda over some art materials. When asked what was wrong, Roberta replied, "She (Vanda) isn't fair. I share, and she doesn't. I'm never letting her have my things again!" The teacher did not dialogue with Roberta at this time. She recognized that Roberta was justifiably upset and would be able to problem solve by herself when she calmed down. In fact, she did just that.

Finally, just because your goal is to dialogue problem situations, this does not mean that you must never become angry yourself. Although angry displays should of course not be the predominant way in which you solve problems with or between children, anger is an emotion with which children must learn to cope, and your showing it occasionally is natural.

## ICPS RESEARCH SUMMARY

Ninety-two children (47 boys, 45 girls) were studied in both grades 5 and 6 (Shure, 1984).* The primary aims of this research were to study the impact of interpersonal ICPS training beginning at age 10 in grade 5 as compared to ICPS training earlier in life at ages 4 and 5, and to compare ICPS training with impersonal Piagetian Critical Thinking (CT) skills in grades 5 and 6. Children trained in grade 5 only or in grades 5 and 6 in either the ICPS or CT groups were comparable in behavioral adjustment and ICPS test scores prior to the interventions in grade 5.

- With pretest scores, IQ, and academic ability controlled, ICPS-trained youngsters gained significantly more than CT-trained controls in the trained ICPS skills of alternative solutions, consequential thinking, and means-ends thinking (sequential planning skills), as measured at the end of grade 5, and maintained those gains through grade 6, especially the two-year trained ICPS group in alternative solutions and means-ends thinking.

- Positive, prosocial behaviors (e.g., being liked by others, caring, sharing, cooperating, showing concern for the feelings of others in distress)

* Shure, M. B. (1984). *Problem solving and mental health of 10- to 12-year-olds* (Final Report No. 35989). Washington, DC: National Institute of Mental Health.

significantly improved in ICPS- vs. CT-trained youngsters whether rated by teachers, peers, or independent observers.

- Impulsive peer-rated behaviors (e.g., aggression, overemotionality, and impatience) decreased in the two-year ICPS- vs. CT-trained groups by the end of grade 6 in both sexes, more dramatically in girls.

- Shy peer-rated behaviors were significantly lower in ICPS- vs. CT-trained youngsters at the end of grade 6 for both boys and girls.

- Linkage analyses support the notion that ICPS skills, particularly solution skills, are significant mediators of behavior change, especially as rated by peers, and most powerfully for prosocial behaviors. That is, ICPS-trained youngsters who most improved in solution skills also most improved in the extent to which they are liked and sought out by peers, and show concern for others in distress.

While it took only one three-month exposure to decrease *negative* behaviors in preschool and kindergarten, it took a repeated exposure in grades 5 and 6 to decrease these behaviors in older children. However, some *negative* behaviors *increased* in CT controls from grades 5 to 6, again suggesting a preventive impact of ICPS intervention.

While it may take longer to affect negative than positive behaviors in older children, it is not too late for ICPS to have beneficial impact on children's mental health and early high-risk behaviors at age 10 or 11.

Standardized achievement test scores and reading-grade levels also improved, suggesting that less stress fostered by ICPS skills allows children to concentrate better on the task-oriented demands of the classroom and subsequently do better in school.

## Significance of ICPS Research

Impulsivity consists of aggression and the inability to delay gratification and cope with frustration, which are significant predictors of later, more serious problems such as violence (a form of hurting others) and substance abuse (a form of hurting oneself). Inhibition consists of the inability to stand up for one's rights and timidity and fear of other children, which are significant predictors of later depression and other forms of mental health dysfunction. ICPS intervention can provide children with skills to think about how to solve problems when they are very young, thus reducing and preventing these early high-risk behaviors in ways that will increase their chance of success and social competence in later years.

---

This research was conducted with low-income, primarily African American populations and funded by the Applied Research Branch and the Prevention Research Branch, National Institute of Mental Health. Research by others nationwide has now replicated the impact of ICPS on a diversity of lower- and middle-income groups, including Caucasian, Hispanic, Asian, and Native American children, as well as with special needs groups, including ADHD and Asperger's Disorder.

For information about additional research by Myrna B. Shure and George Spivack, as well as by others, contact:

Myrna B. Shure, Ph.D.
Drexel University MS 626
245 N. 15th St.
Philadelphia, PA 19102

Phone: (215) 762-7205
Fax: (215) 762-8625
Email: mshure@drexel.edu

# PRE-PROBLEM-SOLVING SKILLS

# Teacher Script

*If the group has had no previous experience with ICPS, use Version 1. If some or all of the children have had ICPS training in an earlier grade, use Version 2.*

**Version 1**

For the next couple of months, we're going to do some things together from a program called ICPS. For us, this means I Can Problem Solve. *(Write these words on chalkboard or easel.)*

The kinds of problems we're going to talk about are the kinds that come up between people—maybe one person wants something another person has, or a child and a teacher are disagreeing about something.

All of us at times have these kinds of problems, and some of them are harder to solve than others. No matter how good we are at solving problems like these, we can all get better at it. We know that the better we can solve problems, the less people feel they have to tell us what to do—and we all like to be able to think things through for ourselves, right? *(Let class respond.)*

Good problem solvers can feel proud to say, "I'm an ICPS kid because I Can Problem Solve." In our ICPS program, we're going to start with some activities that will help you think about other people and how you and other people feel about things. Understanding these things will help you solve problems later on. Some of the ICPS activities are games, and some are more like exercises—all made up to help you think about people.

We're going to make ICPS a part of our class now, and today we're going to start with a game. In this game, you just look around the room and notice things about your classmates. Are you ready?

*Proceed to Lesson 1.*

## Version 2

Many of you have done some things before from a program called ICPS. Who can remember what the letters ICPS mean? *(Let children respond.)*

Very good. You remember. *(Write "I Can Problem Solve" on chalkboard or easel.)*

Who can tell us some kinds of problems that ICPS helps to solve? *(Let children respond.)*

OK, ICPS is about problems that come up between people—other kids or parents or teachers or any people. This year we're going to do some more things from ICPS. All of us at times have these kinds of problems, and some of them are harder to solve than others. No matter how good we are at this, we can all get better, right? *(Let children respond.)*

If you didn't have this program before, it's OK. You'll get the idea of the activities as we go along. And those of you who did this before can help the rest of us, OK? Can someone who had this program before tell us why it is important to be able to solve problems that come up between people?

*If needed:* What did you learn to think about when these kinds of problems came up?

*If still needed:* What do we call ways to solve a problem? *(solutions)*

What do we call what might happen next? *(consequences)*

What do we call words like HAPPY, SAD, and ANGRY? *(feelings)*

If you had ICPS before, think of a recent problem you had with someone and tell us how you solved it. *(Let a child or two respond.)*

Did you solve it differently than you might have before you had ICPS? *(Encourage responses.)*

OK, let's start. Are you ready?

*Proceed to Lesson 1.*

# Who Am I Thinking Of?

## PURPOSE

To encourage children to think about others' characteristics, a first step toward thinking outside oneself when interpersonal problems arise

To focus on negation (IS-NOT) and multiple possibilities (OR-AND) through word concepts children already know, for later ability to think, "I can do this OR that" or "I can do this AND that" in light of whether an idea IS or is NOT a good one

## MATERIALS

None

## TEACHER SCRIPT

Our first ICPS game is called Who Am I Thinking Of?

You have to listen very carefully for this, OK?

*(Keep up a fast, exciting pace.)* I am thinking of someone in this room (for example, in the first two rows).

I am thinking of a girl.

If I am thinking of a girl, name *one* child that I am NOT thinking of. *(Let children respond.)*

Good, I am NOT thinking of (Child 1) because (Child 1) IS a boy.

Who else am I NOT thinking of?

Right, I am NOT thinking of (Child 2) because (Child 2) IS also a boy.

OK, I am thinking of a girl.

I am NOT thinking of someone who IS wearing a (blue dress).

What girl am I NOT thinking of?

*(If two or more girls are wearing blue dresses)* Who else am I NOT thinking of?

*(Name something at least two girls are wearing.)* I am thinking of a girl who IS wearing a (white blouse).

What girls are wearing (white blouses)?

I am thinking of a girl who has on a (white blouse) AND a (red skirt).

Who am I NOT thinking of that has on a (white blouse)?

Who am I thinking of?

OK. I'm going to make this game a little harder now.

*Pick something that at least three children are wearing—for example, two boys and one girl, all wearing green slacks.*

I am thinking of someone with (green slacks) on.

Who am I NOT thinking of?

Good, I am NOT thinking of (Child 3) because (he/she) has (red) slacks on.

I am thinking of a boy with (green slacks) on.

I might be thinking of _____ OR _____. *(Let children answer.)*

I am thinking of a boy who has (green slacks) on but who is NOT wearing a (blue shirt).

I am thinking of _____.

Now I'm thinking of a girl.

I am NOT thinking of a girl whose first name starts with the letter *(L)*.

Who am I NOT thinking of?

Good, I am NOT thinking of (Louise) because (Louise) starts with an *(L)*.

*(If another girl's name starts with the letter you chose)* Who else am I NOT thinking of?

*Pick the first letter in the name of two or more girls.*

I'm thinking of a girl whose first name starts with the letter *(T)*.

I might be thinking of _____ OR _____ *(Let children respond.)*

OK. I'm thinking of a girl whose first name starts with *(T)* AND whose last name starts with *(S)*.

You know, whose initials are (T. S.).

Who am I thinking of?

*Let a child or two think of someone and lead the game as time and interest permit.*

# What Am I Thinking Of?

## PURPOSE

To promote further sensitivity toward and awareness of others

To use the ICPS words SAME-DIFFERENT, in order to help children later think, "That is the SAME idea" and "I can think of something DIFFERENT to do (or say)"

To use the ICPS words SOME-ALL so children can later think, "This solution may work with SOME people but not ALL"

## MATERIALS

None

## TEACHER SCRIPT

OK. Now we're going to change the game we played before.

Are (Child 1) AND (Child 2) wearing the SAME color top OR a DIFFERENT color top?

Who has on the SAME color top as (Child 1)?

OK, now we're going to play a guessing game.

In our last ICPS game, I thought of *people*. Now I'm thinking about *things*.

I'm going to tell children to stand up who ALL have something about them that is the SAME.

*Name all the girls in the group, asking each one to stand up.*

What about ALL the children standing up is the SAME?

How are the children sitting down DIFFERENT from those who are standing up?

*Name all the children who are wearing a certain color, asking each one to stand up. If necessary, tell children that your choice does not depend on whether someone is a boy or a girl.*

How are the children sitting down DIFFERENT from those who are standing up? (*If needed:* It is something that ALL the children who are standing are wearing.)

*If desired, make the game more difficult by naming all the children who are NOT wearing sneakers.*

> What do ALL the children standing up NOT have on that those sitting down do have on?
>
> Now I'm going to make this even harder: I'm going to think of two things that ALL the children I call on have.

*Use, for example, a red shirt and white socks.*

> SOME children sitting down have (red shirts) on.
>
> ALL those standing up have on (red shirts) AND (white socks).

*Think of three, four, and five things, if the group can be so challenged. Let a child lead the group. If necessary, have the child whisper in your ear what he or she is doing so you can help.*

> I'm going to point to two things that are the SAME.
>
> You tell me how they are the SAME.

*Point to two things that are, for example, red or square.*

> Now you point to two things that are the SAME. NOT what I just did.
>
> Then I'll guess how they are the SAME.
>
> Now I'll point to three things that are the SAME, and you tell me how they are the SAME.

*Expand as far as the group can handle. Have a child point to two, three, or four things. Have him or her whisper to you how they are the SAME.*

> Is there someone in this room who has the SAME first name as you?
>
> Does anyone have the SAME last name as you?
>
> Is there someone whose first name begins with the SAME sound (letter) as yours? *(Give an example, if necessary.)*
>
> How about your last name? SAME first letter?

# Two Things at the Same Time

## PURPOSE

To appreciate that people cannot always do two things at the SAME TIME

## MATERIALS

None

## TEACHER SCRIPT

Now we're going to play the Two Things at the Same Time Game.

I'm going to fold my arms AND cross my legs at the SAME TIME, like this. *(Demonstrate.)*

I can do other things at the SAME TIME.

I can raise my hand AND stamp my foot at the SAME TIME, like this. *(Demonstrate.)*

I can laugh AND rub my tummy at the SAME TIME, see, like this. *(Demonstrate.)*

(To Child 1) Come up here and show me two things you can do at the SAME TIME.

_____ AND _____.

*Ask several children to show what two things they can do at the same time. If one child imitates another, ask, "Can you think of two DIFFERENT things you can do at the SAME TIME?"*

(To the group) There are SOME things I can NOT do at the SAME TIME.

I can NOT talk, like this—Hello!—AND sing, like this—La, la, la!—at the SAME TIME.

What two things can you NOT do at the SAME TIME?

*If needed:* Laugh AND _____.

*If still needed:* Can you laugh *(laugh)* AND scream *(scream)* at the SAME TIME? No, you can NOT laugh AND scream at the SAME TIME.

I can NOT talk AND sing at the SAME TIME. *(Demonstrate.)*

Who can think of two DIFFERENT things you can NOT do at the SAME TIME? (*If needed:* Walk AND sit, play tennis AND bowl.)

Can I teach you arithmetic AND spelling at the SAME TIME?

Can I teach ALL of you arithmetic AND talk to one of you who is bothering someone else at the SAME TIME?

If I call on one of you, and ALL of you shout out at the SAME TIME, can I hear the person I called on?

What else can I NOT do at the SAME TIME?
(*For example:* Talk to you AND talk to a guest at the door, listen to you AND to four other children.)

What can you do at the SAME TIME in class?
(*For example:* Sit in your seat AND listen to me.)

What can you NOT do in class at the SAME TIME?
(*For example:* Talk to your friend AND work on your lesson.)

# What Makes People Feel the Way They Do? Part I

## PURPOSE

To sensitize children to people's feelings and preferences by helping them sec that (1) DIFFERENT people can feel DIFFERENT ways about the SAME thing and (2) DIFFERENT people can feel the SAME way about the SAME thing

To use the ICPS feeling word HAPPY so children can later ask, "What can I do so someone will feel HAPPY?"

## MATERIALS

Chalkboard or easel

People List

## TEACHER SCRIPT

---

**NOTE**

You may find it useful to make a poster of the People List on page 25 for use in future lessons.

---

### Part 1

Today's ICPS game is about what makes people feel the way they do.

*Write the word HAPPY on the chalkboard.*

You all know what makes people feel HAPPY. *(Use a happy voice and expression.)*

_____, can you think of something that makes someone HAPPY?

*If the idea is relevant, say, "That's one thing," and write it on the board. If an answer appears to be irrelevant, ask the child who gave it why or how that would make someone happy. The answer may actually turn out to be relevant.*

Now the idea of this game is to think of lots of DIFFERENT things that can make people HAPPY.

If you can think of something DIFFERENT that can make someone HAPPY, raise your hand.

*Continue until seven or eight children have answered, writing all responses on the board. Then classify enumerations, or variations on the same theme. Some common enumerations are as follows.*

*Going somewhere:* To the zoo, the park, a movie

*Receiving a present:* A skateboard, a new shirt, a game

*Eating certain kinds of food:* Chocolate cake, ice cream, pizza

*To point out an enumeration, you might say, for example, "Chocolate cake and ice cream are both kinds of food. Can you think of something DIFFERENT from food that might make someone feel HAPPY?"*

DIFFERENT people can feel the SAME way about the SAME thing—or DIFFERENT ways about the SAME thing.

## Part 2

Now we're going to talk about what makes *you* feel HAPPY.

If riding a skateboard makes you feel HAPPY, raise your hand.

Those who have their hands up feel the SAME way about the SAME thing.

If riding a skateboard does NOT make you feel HAPPY, raise your hand.

SOME of you feel HAPPY about riding a skateboard and SOME of you do NOT.

DIFFERENT people can feel DIFFERENT ways about the SAME thing.

Is that OK?

Yes, it's OK for DIFFERENT people to feel DIFFERENT ways about the SAME thing.

*If all the children raise their hands, just say, "Oh, that makes ALL of you HAPPY." Continue to ask about various items and activities until someone says he or she would not be happy.*

**Part 3**

Now I'm going to make a list of DIFFERENT people, and you tell me things that might make these people feel HAPPY.

They can be things already mentioned *(point to ideas already on the board)*, or they can be new things.

Try to think of something DIFFERENT for each person.

*Write the following list on the board.*

### People List

1. A mother
2. A teacher
3. A fire fighter
4. A father
5. A 4-year-old child
6. A grandmother
7. A boy or girl your age

*To maximize participation, call on individual children to say what might make a different person on the People List feel happy.*

Now, if you can think of something that would make at least *two* of these people feel HAPPY—that is, the SAME thing that might make DIFFERENT people feel HAPPY—raise your hand.

*Let as many children answer as time and interest permit. Ask each respondent to identify the people he or she is referring to. If not already given, ask:*

Can you think of something a boy or girl your age could do that would make at least *two* of these people HAPPY?

It could be something you might do, or it could be something another person your age might do.

---

**HINT**

In classifying, you can use the word *enumeration*. Children come to understand this word, and they enjoy using it. (You may prefer to use the word *variation* instead.)

---

# What Makes People Feel the Way They Do? Part II

## PURPOSE

To use the ICPS feeling word ANGRY so children can later ask, "What can I do so someone else won't be ANGRY?"

## MATERIALS

Chalkboard or easel

People List (from Lesson 4)

## TEACHER SCRIPT

*Write the word ANGRY and the People List on the chalkboard (or refer children to a poster of the People List).*

Are ANGRY and mad the SAME or DIFFERENT feelings?

Yes, the SAME. Mad is just another word for ANGRY.

Today's ICPS game is about the word ANGRY.

### Part 1

*Follow the directions given for Part 1 of Lesson 4, referring children to the People List and asking, "What makes these DIFFERENT people feel ANGRY?"*

### Part 2

*When children can give no further responses, follow the directions for Part 2 of Lesson 4, asking, "What makes you feel ANGRY?"*

## Part 3

*After children have generated all the answers they can, classify enumerations. Some common enumerations are as follows:*

*Hurting someone:* Hitting, kicking, knocking down

*Taking something (borrowing, with the intent to return):* Paper, bike, books

*Taking something (stealing, with no intent to return):* Pen, sweater, hat

*Wrongly accusing:* Said I cheated, said I lied

*Gossiping:* Told someone he doesn't like my clothes, my hair

*To classify enumerations, you might say, for example, "Hitting and kicking are kind of the SAME. They are enumerations because they're variations of the SAME idea—in this case, ways that can hurt. Can you think of something DIFFERENT from hurting that might make someone ANGRY?"*

---

**HINT**

In this lesson, be sure to clarify what a child means by "taking"— that is, whether borrowing or stealing is meant.

---

# What Makes People Feel the Way They Do? Part III

## PURPOSE

To use the ICPS feeling words SAD, AFRAID, and JEALOUS

## MATERIALS

Chalkboard or easel

People List (from Lesson 4)

## TEACHER SCRIPT

*Write the words SAD, AFRAID, and JEALOUS and the People List on the chalkboard (or refer children to a poster of the People List).*

> Today's ICPS game is about the words SAD, AFRAID, and JEALOUS.
>
> Since most of you know what these words mean, here's what we're going to do.
>
> I'm going to ask you to pick a person from the People List, then choose one of the three feeling words—SAD, AFRAID, or JEALOUS.
>
> You then think about what could happen or what someone might do that might make the person you picked feel that way.
>
> For example, a 4-year-old child might feel AFRAID if he hears a loud noise.
>
> Tell us what person you pick and which word you're going to tell us about.
>
> Raise your hand when you're ready.

*If a child's response seems to be illogical or the child does not seem to understand the meaning of the word, ask him or her why or how that would make the person feel that way. If the child's response is still illogical, ask the class what they think about what was just said. Remember to classify enumerations as they are given.*

> **HINT**
>
> For this and Lessons 10, 11, and 14, choose questions your group best responds to or feels most challenged by. You do not need to include each of the three parts from Lesson 4.

# ICPS Concepts: Negation, Multiple Possibilities, Feelings, Two Things at the Same Time

*Try incorporating and building upon individual ICPS concepts in the classroom. This will help you later on when you use ICPS dialoguing in problem situations with children. It will also help children extend learning to real life.*

## SOME HELPFUL QUESTIONS

### During indoor recess:

You are (for example, sitting) AND (playing checkers) at the SAME TIME.

What can you NOT do at the SAME TIME you are (playing checkers)?

What two things IS _____ doing at the SAME TIME?

### When you are teaching a lesson:

Am I writing on the board AND teaching you (math) at the SAME TIME?

Can I explain this lesson AND leave the room at the SAME TIME?

I understand your feelings when you have your hand up and I don't call on you. You feel _____.

Can I call on ALL of you at the SAME TIME?

### When a child is doing homework:

How do you feel when you do NOT finish your homework?

What were you doing when you should have been doing your homework?

Can you (go to a party) AND do your homework at the SAME TIME?

### When a child interrupts:

Can I talk to you AND to _____ at the SAME TIME?

How do I feel when you interrupt me?

Can you think of something DIFFERENT to do until I can talk to you?

### When a child shouts out:

Can I call on you AND _____ at the SAME TIME?

If you shout out while I'm listening to _____, how do you think I feel?

### When a child is talking to others during a lesson:

(Child 1), can you talk to (Child 2) AND hear what I'm saying at the SAME TIME?

How do you think I feel when you talk while I'm trying to teach you this lesson?

How might you feel later if you do NOT know what I'm teaching?

### When a child makes you or another child feel angry:

How do you think (I/_____) feel(s) now?

Do you know why (I/_____) feel(s) that way?

What can you do so (I/_____) will NOT feel that way?

Do you know why (I/_____) feel(s) ANGRY when you (for example, throw food, interrupt, start a fight, copy someone's homework)?

### When a child disrupts other children in line:

How (do I/does _____) feel when you disrupt the line?

What can you do so (I/_____) won't feel that way?

How do the others feel when we have to wait for you to get into line?

### When a child disrupts the class:

We are ALL doing our (math) work now. What are *you* doing?

Are you doing the SAME thing OR something DIFFERENT?

*ICPS can become a verb. One child was heard to say to another, "You should ICPS" and another, "You're not ICPSing." You can ask, when appropriate, "Are you ICPSing?"*

## MINI-DIALOGUES

*These mini-dialogues show how different people can feel different ways about the same thing and illustrate use of the concept "Two things at the SAME TIME," taught in Lesson 3.*

**Situation 1:** DeMarcus returns to his homeroom from science class.

DeMarcus: Ms. Brown [the science teacher] wouldn't let me finish my milk.

Teacher: Why do you think that happened?

DeMarcus: I don't know.

Teacher: What was everybody else doing?

DeMarcus: Looking at the science projects. But I was, too.

Teacher: So you were looking at the projects AND finishing your milk at the SAME TIME?

DeMarcus: That's right.

Teacher: Could there be a problem with that?

DeMarcus: Well, you let us work and eat in *here.*

Teacher: Why wouldn't Ms. Brown like that?

DeMarcus: I don't know.

Teacher: Is looking at the science projects AND drinking milk at the SAME TIME a good idea? What might happen?

DeMarcus: Well, milk could spill on them.

Teacher: Who else has to look at the projects?

DeMarcus: All the kids.

Teacher: Now do you see how Ms. Brown and I can feel DIFFERENT ways about eating AND working at the SAME TIME?

*Whenever a situation arises that elicits the feelings of at least two people, positive or negative, you can ask the child to identify both his or her own and others' feelings. Then ask, "Do you think you feel the SAME way OR a DIFFERENT way about this?"*

**Situation 2:** Joan is pushing her way to the front of the line to the drinking fountain.

Teacher:   Joan, how do you think the others feel when you get in front of them like that?

Joan:   Mad at me.

Teacher:   Do you think they feel the SAME way OR a DIFFERENT way than you do about it?

Joan:   Different.

Teacher:   Can you think of something DIFFERENT to do so the others won't feel mad at you?

*Giving the initiative back to the child creates a very different mood than demands or threats. However, if a child is very emotional, it is generally better to wait and talk about the situation later.*

# ICPS Concepts: What Am I Thinking Of? Negation, Multiple Possibilities, Feelings

*The examples of ICPS concepts integrated in the curriculum reflect a range of levels of academic ability throughout the intermediate grades. Choose those activities appropriate for your class.*

## READING AND STORY COMPREHENSION

I am thinking of a character in the story _____.

I am thinking of a (for example, girl).

I am NOT thinking of _____.

I am thinking of a (girl) who (for example, talked to the clowns).

I might be thinking of _____ OR _____ OR _____.

I am thinking of a (girl) who did (talk to the clowns) but who did NOT (for example, get the attention she wanted).

I am thinking of _____.

How do you think _____ felt about _____?

Why do you think (he/she) felt that way?

Did two people feel a DIFFERENT way about the SAME thing?

## MATH

I am thinking of something in this room that IS (round).

What am I NOT thinking of?

I am thinking of something that IS (round) AND red.

What am I thinking of?

*(After a correct guess)* Good thinking! How does that make you feel?

I am thinking of an object that is NOT on *your* right.
(*If needed:* IS on *my* right.)

I am thinking of an object that is NOT brown.

I am thinking of an object that IS red but is NOT round.

What am I thinking of?

*Point to things in the room that are the same in some way (color, shape, function, and so forth), as in Lesson 2.*

I am thinking of a combination of numbers that equals 10.

I am NOT thinking of a combination that contains a 7.

I am NOT thinking of $7 + 3$ OR $7 + 2 + 1$ OR $(10 - 7) + 7$.

I am also NOT thinking of $7^2 - 39$.

What else am I NOT thinking of? *(Elicit many responses.)*

I am thinking of a combination that has the number 8.

I am NOT thinking of $8 + 2$ OR $(8 - 4) + 6$ OR $3^2 - 1 + 2$.

*Encourage children to guess until they come up with $(8 - 3) + 5$, then let them make up examples of their own.*

I am thinking of SOME coins that equal 50 cents.

I am NOT thinking of a quarter, 3 nickels, and 10 pennies.

I am thinking of a combination that has a quarter, but does NOT have a nickel.

I might be thinking of _____ OR _____ OR _____.

*Let the group guess until they say 1 quarter, 1 dime, and 15 pennies.*

## Happy

Would you feel happier if your basketball team got:

a. $\dfrac{222}{111}$ points, and your opponent got $\dfrac{500}{400}$ points?

OR

b. $2 \times 65$ points, and your opponent got $355 - 240$ points?

Would you feel happier if you could buy:

**Example 1**

a. 1 pint

OR

b. 1 quart

OR

c. 1 cup of your favorite ice cream?

**Example 2**

a. 7 pints

OR

b. 3 quarts

OR

c. 9 pints

OR

d. 1 gallon of your favorite ice cream?


Would you feel happier if you were a long jumper, and you just jumped:

**Example 1**

a. $\dfrac{20}{2}$ + 2 feet

OR

b. 3 yards + 1 foot?

**Example 2**

a. 5 yards − 2 feet

OR

b. 72 inches?


Would you be happier if you had:

**Example 1**

a. 5 pennies and 10 nickels

OR

b. 1 quarter, 1 dime, and 5 pennies?

**Example 2**

a. 2,000 + 1,700 + 40 + 2 pennies

OR

b. 3,840 pennies?

Would you be happier if you could do your favorite activity for:

**Example 1**

a. $\frac{1}{4} + \frac{1}{4}$ of an hour

OR

b. $\frac{1}{2} + \frac{1}{4}$ of an hour

OR

c. $\frac{1}{3}$ of an hour minus 5 minutes?

**Example 2**

a. XXIV minutes

OR

b. XIV minutes

**Example 3**

a. $3^2 \times 3$ minutes

OR

b. $3^3$ minutes?

Would you be happier if you had a pizza and could have:

**Example 1**

a. $\frac{3}{4}$ of a piece

OR

b. $\frac{2}{5}$ of a piece?

**Example 2**

a. $\frac{5}{8} - \frac{1}{3}$ of a piece

OR

b. $\frac{.48}{6}$ of a piece

OR

c. $\frac{.48}{0.6}$ of a piece?

**Example 3**

a. $\frac{1}{3}$ of 18 pieces

OR

b. $\frac{1}{4}$ of 20 pieces?

## Angry

Would you be angrier if someone was late by:

a. $\frac{.048}{.06}$ minutes

OR

b. $\frac{.048}{0.6}$ minutes?

*Let the group make up examples of their own.*

## Sad

Something you want costs $15.00. Would you feel saddest if you had:

a. $\frac{1}{3}$ of its cost $\times$ 3

OR

b. $\frac{2}{3}$ of its cost $+$ 6

OR

c. $\left(\frac{2}{5}$ of its cost $\times 2\right) + 4$?

*Continue to let children make up their own examples.*

## SCIENCE

I am thinking of a plant, but NOT a red plant.

I am NOT thinking of _____.

I am thinking of a plant that IS green AND has long leaves.

I am NOT thinking of a (cactus).

I am thinking of a plant whose leaves have a yellow-green border AND dark green spots.

I am NOT thinking of _____.

I am thinking of _____.

*Use color, size, texture, odor, and so forth for distinguishing criteria. Let the class think of other examples, such as animals who do or do not live in water or in the desert, who do or do not eat grass, and so forth.*

## SOCIAL STUDIES

I am thinking of someone who was President of the United States.

He was NOT President after 1950.

Who am I NOT thinking of?

I am thinking of a President whose last name was Adams.

I am thinking of _____ OR _____.

I am NOT thinking of the second President of the United States.

Who am I thinking of?

*Use what the class has studied to identify any public figure in history, sports, entertainment, and so forth.*

## GEOGRAPHY

I am thinking of a continent.

I am thinking of a continent that the equator crosses.

I am thinking of _____ OR _____.

I am NOT thinking of a continent where people speak Swahili.

I am thinking of _____.

I am thinking of a city in the eastern United States.

I am NOT thinking of _____.

I am thinking of a city in the state of New York.

I am NOT thinking of its capital.

I am NOT thinking of _____.

I am thinking of a city that has the Empire State Building.
(*If needed:* AND that has Madison Square Garden.)

I am thinking of _____.

# Telephone Message

## PURPOSE

To show that one must listen carefully to what people say, in order to help prevent later faulty communication in problem solving

## MATERIALS

None

## TEACHER SCRIPT

*Select a group of six or seven players to participate in this familiar game:*

1. Instruct the players to leave the room, then tell your message to the remaining children.

   *Possible messages:*  I can fly in the sky like Superman, but I've got 14 arms and 16 eyes, and that's not a lie.

   I live in a tree, but I'm not a squirrel, and I don't twirl around much around purple flowers.

2. Have the players return and sit in a circle.

3. Whisper a message quickly into Player 1's ear.

4. Have Player 1 whisper the message to Player 2. Have Player 2 whisper to Player 3, and so forth.

5. Ask the last player to tell the message he or she heard to the class. It is likely that the last player will hear a message quite different from the one you relayed to the first player.

*Ask the group if they can think of two reasons why you had them play the game. If needed, ask, "What might happen if you don't listen to what someone tells you?" If "I'd get in trouble" is the response, say, "Tell us more about that."*

If someone tells you something someone else said, is it a good idea to find out for yourself?

Why?

How can you find out what the person really said?

Can you think of a time when someone told you something that someone else said that turned out NOT to be true?

What happened then?

How can getting the message help to avoid a problem—you know, keep it from happening in the first place?

*If not everyone in the group is able to participate as a player, explain that those who did not will get a turn in other lessons.*

## OPTIONS

1. Choose a new team of players and repeat the game with a new message. A player can make up his or her own message, if desired.

2. Divide the class into small groups, each transmitting the same message simultaneously. Whisper the message to the first player in each group but tell the last player to wait until all groups are finished to report to the class. It will be interesting to hear the different ways each group heard the message.

# Did I Get the Whole Message?

## PURPOSE

To reinforce the idea that one must listen carefully to what people say, in order to help prevent later faulty communication in problem solving

## MATERIALS

Mini-Play 1

## TEACHER SCRIPT

---

**NOTE**

Make a copy of Mini-Play 1 for each actor, then circle each actor's part. If desired, you may make name tags for each actor in this and subsequent lessons involving mini-plays.

---

We're going to have an ICPS mini-play today, and I will need three boys to play parts.

The rest of you listen carefully because you may have a chance to make up a scene.

*Choose three boys to read Mini-Play 1. If a boy has a yellow shirt on, choose him for the part of William. Play the part of the teacher yourself.*

*When the mini-play is completed, ask the following questions:*

What was Robert's whole message?

What message did Samuel give to William?

*(To the child playing Samuel)* Samuel, what might have happened when you gave William only part of the message?
*(If needed:* What might William have said or done?*)*

*(To the child playing William)* William, how did you feel before you got the whole message?

How do you feel now?

(To the group) What did you learn from this?

How could this problem have been avoided?
(If needed: By getting the whole _____.)

*Let three new children have a chance to make up another mini-play illustrating the importance of getting the whole message. Give them a few minutes to plan in a corner of the room or in the hallway, then ask them to perform. Discuss with the class when complete.*

## THE WHOLE MESSAGE

Robert: Hi, Samuel. You know what? I don't like yellow walls. They give me a stomachache. *(Sits down.)*

Samuel: *(To William)* William, Robert doesn't like your new shirt. It's yellow, and it gives him a stomachache.

William: I'm going to get him. He'll be sorry he said that.

Teacher: What are you so mad about, William?

William: Robert doesn't like my new shirt.

Teacher: How do you know that?

William: Samuel told me.

Teacher: Do you remember the Telephone Message Game we played?

William: Yeah.

Teacher: Are you sure you got the *whole* message?

William: That's what Samuel said.

Teacher: How can you find out if Samuel got the whole message?

William: Ask Robert.

William: *(To Robert)* Robert, did you tell Samuel you don't like my shirt?

Robert: What? Why would I say that?

William: 'Cause yellow gives you a stomachache.

Robert: That's not what I said. I said yellow *walls* give me a stomachache.

Samuel: I'm sorry, William. I thought he just said yellow.

# The Whole Message

**MINI-DIALOGUE**

**Situation:** Joyce gets inaccurate information from Sandra.

Joyce: *(To the teacher)* Jamie's going to beat me up after school.

Teacher: How do you know that?

Joyce: Sandra told me.

Teacher: Do you remember the Telephone Message Game we played?

Joyce: Yeah.

Teacher: Are you sure you got the *whole* message?

Joyce: That's what Sandra said.

Teacher: How can you find out if Sandra got the whole message?

Joyce: Ask Jamie.

*Later . . .*

Joyce: *(To the teacher)* Jamie's not going to beat me up.

Teacher: What happened?

Joyce: She said she was going to beat me up if I didn't give her back her paper, so I gave it back to her.

Teacher: What did you learn from this?

Joyce: To get the whole message.

Teacher: How did you feel before you got the whole message?

Joyce: Scared . . . and worried.

Teacher: How do you feel now?

Joyce: Happy . . . and relieved.

# Are You Listening to Me? Part I

## PURPOSE

To give children practice listening to others, in order to encourage later sensitivity to others' thoughts and feelings

## MATERIALS

Mini-Plays 2–4

## TEACHER SCRIPT

---
**NOTE**

Make a copy of Mini-Plays 2–4 for each actor. Circle each actor's part.

---

### Mini-Play 2

I need two children to act out another ICPS mini-play.
This one is a Silly Skit.

*Choose two generally verbal children to perform the first mini-play. After the performance, ask the following:*

There's something silly about the way these two kids were talking to each other. Can you figure out what it is?

*If the response relates to content (for example, "Tomorrow's not her mother's birthday"), prompt by saying, "No, it's not what he said, it's how they're talking to each other." If needed, say, "When A says, 'My knee is bleeding' and B answers, 'Tomorrow is my mother's birthday,' does A think B IS or is NOT listening?"*

Who IS B thinking of?

And A?

What could B say OR ask that would show (he/she) heard what A said?

*Have a child who responds appropriately come up and play the part of B. Ask for another actor to play the part of A.*

*(To the new actors)* OK, now A, say, "My knee is bleeding."

And B, say something to show you listened to A.

Make up the rest so it's NOT silly—a NOT silly skit.

Keep going until you think the scene is finished.

## Mini-Play 3

Now there's going to be another Silly Skit, but in this one there will be a time when we know B IS listening to A.

As soon as you hear B IS listening to A—that is, says something to show (he/she) heard what was said—raise your hand, OK?

Remember, when you hear someone IS listening, raise your hand.

*Select two new actors and have them read the mini-play. If a child raises his or her hand at an inappropriate place, ask why or what made the child think each actor heard what the other said. After the mini-play, ask the following questions:*

Who IS B thinking of?

And A?

What could B say OR ask that would show (he/she) listened to what A said?

*Have a child who responds appropriately come up and play the part of B. Ask for another actor to play the part of A. Encourage B to respond to A in a way that shows he or she is listening and to continue the mini-play in a "NOT silly" way until the end.*

## Mini-Play 4

This mini-play is another Silly Skit, but this time, there's only going to be one place in the story where we know that B heard what A said and answered in a way that makes sense.

Listen carefully, and when you hear that place, raise your hand.

*Choose two new actors to read the mini-play.*

Why is the last thing A said silly?

If A IS listening to B, what might (he/she) say instead?

*Have a child who responds appropriately come up and play the part of B. Ask for another actor to play the part of A. Encourage B to respond to A in a way that shows he or she is listening and to continue the mini-play in a "NOT silly" way until the end.*

**SILLY SKIT**

A:    My knee is bleeding.

B:    Tomorrow is my mother's birthday.

A:    Do you have a bandage?

B:    What do you think I can get her?

A:    I guess I should wash off my knee.

B:    I guess I could get her a toaster.

**SILLY SKIT**

A: I feel sad today.

B: I'm reading a new book.

A: My friend said he'd play with me, and then he said he couldn't.

B: My book is a mystery story.

A: I wish my friend could play today.

B: Why can't he play today?

A: 'Cause he said his mom won't let him.

B: In my book, someone stole a dog.

A: I don't like my friend anymore.

B: I bet you feel angry at him.

A: Yeah, I do.

## SILLY SKIT

A: I got a racing car for Christmas.

B: I don't like blueberries.

A: My racing car is the fastest on the block.

B: My mom made me eat blueberry pie last night.

A: It's red and has a white top.

B: I feel sick today.

A: I got other things, too.

B: I'd rather have chocolate cake.

A: I got a new shirt, too.

B: Mom says that's not good for my teeth.

A: Why not?

B: I'll get cavities and get fat.

A: How could a new shirt make you get cavities and fat?

# Silly Skit Reminders

*When the class is noisy and not listening, say, "My knee is bleeding." This should attract their attention. If not, ask, "Do you remember the Silly Skits? Are you listening to me?"*

### When a child's answer appears unrelated to your question:

*(In a nonthreatening tone)* What do you think the question was?

*If the child correctly repeats the question:* OK, try to answer it again.

*If the child did not hear the question:* Do you remember the Silly Skits? Were you listening to me? OK, I'll repeat the question. Really listen this time.

### When you hear one child responding to another in a way that shows he or she is not listening:

*(To Child 1)* Do you remember the Silly Skits? Did you listen to (Child 2)?

*If (Child 1) knows what (Child 2) said:* How can you answer so (he/she) will know you listened?

*If (Child 1) does not know what (Child 2) said:* OK. Really listen this time. Be sure to answer so (he/she) will know you listened.

*Often children hear what another said but are too consumed by their own interests to respond appropriately.*

# What Makes People Feel the Way They Do? Part IV

## PURPOSE

To help children understand the ICPS feeling words FRUSTRATED, IMPATIENT, LONELY, and SYMPATHETIC, for later coping with these emotions

## MATERIALS

Chalkboard or easel

People List (from Lesson 4)

## TEACHER SCRIPT

*Write the words FRUSTRATED, IMPATIENT, LONELY, and SYMPATHETIC and the People List on the chalkboard (or refer children to a poster of the People List). Direct children's attention to the People List as needed.*

Today we have new feeling words for our ICPS lesson.

You may know SOME but not ALL of them.

If you know a word, tell us what it means, give an example, and tell us what makes *you* feel that way.

FRUSTRATED: When things go wrong, you can't finish something, or you feel helpless

- When a person's shoelace breaks when she's trying to tie it, she feels FRUSTRATED.

- I want to tell Peter something, but he keeps talking. That makes me feel FRUSTRATED.

- When I have to turn off a television show I like in the middle, I feel FRUSTRATED.

- When you have your hand up and I don't call on you, I know you might feel FRUSTRATED.

What else can make someone feel FRUSTRATED?

What makes *you* feel FRUSTRATED?

IMPATIENT: When you feel you can't wait

- I've got to have that candy now. I can't wait till later.
- Sometimes when people feel FRUSTRATED, they also feel IMPATIENT. Martina said, "When Jim wouldn't give me his pencil, I felt FRUSTRATED. So I took it 'cause I was IMPATIENT."

What else can make someone feel IMPATIENT?

What makes *you* feel IMPATIENT?

LONELY: When you wish other people were around when they're not

- LaTanya feels LONELY today because her friends didn't come to play.
- When Grandma left for home today, I felt very LONELY.

What else can make someone feel LONELY?

What makes *you* feel LONELY?

SYMPATHETIC: When you feel sad for someone else

- Ralph really hurt himself when he fell, and I feel SYMPATHETIC towards him.
- LuAnn found out Elizabeth didn't do well on her social studies project, and LuAnn feels SYMPATHETIC.

What else can make someone feel SYMPATHETIC?

What makes *you* feel SYMPATHETIC?

## OPTIONS

1. If some children are having difficulty understanding the feeling words, pair them with classmates who can help. If desired, divide the whole class into pairs to think of examples. Depending upon group progress, either you or the pairs can choose the feeling words and individuals from the People List.

2. Prepare two sets of index cards, one listing the feeling words, the other naming the individuals on the People List. Let children pick a card from each set, then have them give an example of what makes the person chosen feel that way. Children can raise their hands when they are ready. In this way, a child who cannot respond will not feel embarrassed.

# What Makes People Feel the Way They Do? Part V

## PURPOSE

To help children understand the ICPS feeling words ASHAMED, EMBARRASSED, and SURPRISED, for later coping with these emotions

## MATERIALS

Chalkboard or easel

People List (from Lesson 4)

## TEACHER SCRIPT

*Write the words ASHAMED, EMBARRASSED, and SURPRISED and the People List on the chalkboard (or refer children to a poster of the People List). Direct children's attention to the People List as needed.*

Today we're going to talk about the words ASHAMED, EMBARRASSED, and SURPRISED.

*Ask children to define these words and give examples.*

ASHAMED: Being sorry for something you did or said

- I'm sorry I lied to you. I feel ASHAMED.
- Bonita felt ASHAMED of herself when she forgot her best friend's birthday.

What else can make someone feel ASHAMED?

What makes *you* feel ASHAMED?

EMBARRASSED: When you think people are looking at you because you did something silly, feeling ill at ease

- Ray fell on the ice. He feels EMBARRASSED.
- Sometimes people can feel ASHAMED and EMBARRASSED: I'm sorry I accused you of taking my pencil. I feel ASHAMED that I thought that. I also feel EMBARRASSED because you knew you didn't take it, and I said you did.

59

What else can make someone feel EMBARRASSED?

What makes *you* feel EMBARRASSED?

SURPRISED: When something happens that you didn't expect to happen (positive or negative)

- Pamela was SURPRISED to see her friend. She thought she was in New York.

- I'm SURPRISED you did that. You usually don't do things like that.

What else can make someone feel SURPRISED?

What makes *you* feel SURPRISED?

# Are You Listening to Me? Part II

## PURPOSE

To provide additional practice listening to others, in order to encourage later sensitivity to others' thoughts and feelings

## MATERIALS

Mini-Plays 5 and 6

## TEACHER SCRIPT

---

**NOTE**

Make a copy of Mini-Plays 5 and 6 for each actor, then circle each actor's part.

---

Do you remember the Silly Skits we did?

Who remembers what was wrong with the way the two kids were talking to each other? (*If needed:* Was everyone listening?)

Why do you think it is important to listen to people?

*If needed:* If someone says something you need to hear, and you do NOT listen, what might happen?

How do you think the person who is talking feels if you do NOT listen?

Can you think of any other reasons to listen?

### Mini-Play 5

Now I need two actors to perform another Silly Skit.

As soon as you hear one person IS listening to the other—that is, says something to show he or she heard the other person—raise your hand.

*Have the actors read the mini-play. If a child raises a hand at an inappropriate time, be sure to ask why or what made him or her think one person heard what the other said. After the mini-play is complete:*

*(To the actors)* OK, start the mini-play again, with A saying, "My toes are red," but this time show you are listening.

## Mini-Play 6

OK, I need two more actors for another Silly Skit.

Again, raise your hand when you hear that one
person IS listening to the other.

*Select actors and have them perform the mini-play. After they have finished,
have them repeat the performance so it is "NOT silly."*

*Next have the entire group work in pairs, making up their own Silly Skits. As
time and interest permit, let pairs perform their skits for the group. Observers
can raise their hands when they hear one child listening to the other.*

## SAMPLE SILLY SKIT

*This skit was written by a fifth grader.*

> A: It's a shame about my parents.
>
> B: It's so hot.
>
> A: They got a divorce.
>
> B: I wish there was a tree around here.
>
> A: Now I have to live with my mother.
>
> B: Why do you have to live with her?
>
> A: Because my mother got custody of me.
>
> B: Hey, there is the ice-cream man.

## SILLY SKIT

A:  My toes are red.

B:  I got two pet turtles from my mom.

A:  I was out in the snow, and my toes got red.

B:  They crawl funny.

A:  They itch.

B:  One is really, really huge.

A:  Do you have some medicine?

B:  It's green and slimy.

A:  Yucky! I don't like that medicine. I'll just soak my toes.

B:  I'll get you some warm water to soak your toes.

A:  Thanks.

## SILLY SKIT

A:   I feel frustrated today.

B:   I got new shoes for my birthday.

A:   I've blown up five balloons, and they all popped.

B:   My shoes are white with brown tips.

A:   I have two blue balloons and three yellow balloons.

B:   I wish my shoes were red with pink tips.

A:   I wish I could blow them up without popping.

B:   That's hard to do.

A:   I know. You have to be careful.

B:   How can you blow up shoes, anyway?

# Do You Remember? Part I

## PURPOSE

To provide more practice in paying attention and remembering what people say about things, with a focus on personal preferences

## MATERIALS

Chalkboard or easel

## TEACHER SCRIPT

The ICPS game for today is Do You Remember?

To play, we need two teams.

Everyone on this side of the room *(point to your right side)* is on Team A.

All of you on this side *(point to your left side)* are on Team B.

I will need seven of you from each team to be the panel—the rest of you will be the players.

The idea of the game is for the players to remember what the panel members say.

*Divide the class into the two teams, as shown.*

| **Team A** | **Team B** |
|---|---|
| Panel (standing up) | Panel (standing up) |
| O  O  O  O  O  O  O | O  O  O  O  O  O  O |
| | |
| Players (at desks) | Players (at desks) |
| X  X  X  X | X  X  X  X |
| X  X  X | X  X  X |

*After the groups have been organized:*

> First I'm going to ask the panel for Team A to tell us, one at a time, a food they like a lot.
>
> Now all you players on Team A *(point to the players),* try to remember what each panel member says.
>
> Team B, you wait because it will be your turn to do this next, only we'll change the question.
>
> Team A will get a point for everything one of their players remembers.
>
> Whichever team has the most points will win the game.
>
> And the next time we play this game, other kids will be on the panel.
>
> *(To each of the Team A panel members)* _____, what food do you like a lot?

*Ask the seven panel members in sequence, jotting down their names and the foods identified as they answer. It is all right if two or three panel members name the same food, but if more do so, ask them to think of a different one.*

*If a panel member takes too long in answering, tell him or her to think about it, go on to the next child, and return to the first child at the end.*

*If a child is generally shy and nonresponsive, you can suggest that he or she name the same thing as another child. This will help the child participate.*

> *(To Team A players)* Who can remember SOME or ALL of the foods your team's panel said they liked?
>
> You have to say who named the food: For example, (Tom) said he liked (pizza).

*Verify the players' answers against your list of panel members and foods named. Tally each correct answer on the chalkboard. If the first player does not remember all seven panel members' choices, ask another player from the same team to continue.*

> *(To Team B panel members)* OK, each of you tell us what sport or game you like.

*Record Team B panel members' answers and verify and tally Team B players' correct answers as before.*

> *(To Team A panel members)* Here's round two. Each of you tell us what animal you like.

*Record Team A panel members' answers and verify and tally Team A players' correct answers as before. Be sure to choose a different Team A player to begin naming the Team A panel members and their chosen animals.*

(To Team B panel members) Each of you tell us which television show you like.

*Record Team B panel members' answers and verify and tally Team B players' correct answers as before. Choose a different Team B player to begin naming the Team B panel members and their chosen television shows.*

(To the class) OK, now I'm going to change the game a little.

Each panel member is going to tell us again what he or she said before, and then I'm going to ask the players the questions a little differently.

Try to remember what your team says.

(To Team A panel members) Each of you tell us again what food you said you like.

Now, what animal did each of you like?

Now, tell us what food each of you does NOT like.

*Record answers as before.*

(To Team A players) Raise your hand if you remember who said they like _____.

*Name a food, then tally on the board if the answer is correct. If incorrect, ask if anyone else on the team remembers.*

Who said they do NOT like _____? (Name a food.)

What animal does (Child 1) like?

Does anyone else on your panel like the SAME animal?

What food did (Child 2) say (he/she) did NOT like?

What animal did (Child 2) AND (Child 3) say they like?

*Tally correct answers. If the Team A players remember everything, create questions involving what three or four panel members said. If the questions are still too easy, add more, such as panel members' birthday month or date.*

(To Team B panel members) Each of you tell us again what sport or game you like.

Now what television show you like.

Now tell us what television show you do NOT like.

(To Team B players) Raise your hand if you remember who said they like _____. (Name a sport or game.)

*Tally each correct answer.*

Who said they like _____. *(Name a television show.)*

Did anyone else say they like the SAME television show?

Who said they do NOT like the SAME television show?

What television show did _____ AND _____ say
they do NOT like?

*As for Team A, increase questions if necessary. Just be sure each team has an
equal number of questions so a final score can be tallied.*

---

**HINT**

Increase the number of panel members as far as your class can be
challenged. You can use birthday month, favorite color, and the like
as categories, or let children choose their own categories.

---

# What Makes People Feel the Way They Do? Part VI

## PURPOSE

To use the ICPS feeling words DISAPPOINTED, PROUD, WORRIED, and RELIEVED, in order to help children think further about their impact on others

## MATERIALS

Chalkboard or easel

People List (from Lesson 4)

## TEACHER SCRIPT

*Write the words DISAPPOINTED, PROUD, WORRIED, and RELIEVED and the People List on the chalkboard (or refer children to a poster of the People List). Direct children's attention to the People List as needed.*

Today's ICPS lesson is about some more feeling words.

When I tell you the word, raise your hand if you can tell us what the word means.

Then give an example of it and tell us what makes *you* feel that way.

DISAPPOINTED: When something you want or hope for doesn't happen

- Robert felt DISAPPOINTED when he wasn't picked for the basketball team.

- People can also feel DISAPPOINTED in others: Susan was DISAPPOINTED in Jennie when she didn't keep her promise.

What else can make someone feel DISAPPOINTED?

What makes *you* feel DISAPPOINTED?

PROUD: When someone does something very well,
a feeling of self-satisfaction

- Sarah won first prize and feels very PROUD of herself.
- You can feel PROUD of someone else, too: Janette's mother
  felt PROUD of Janette when she _____.

What else can make someone feel PROUD?

What makes *you* feel PROUD?

WORRIED: Thinking and feeling uneasy about something you either
want or don't want to happen

- Tom wants to pass his spelling test, but he's WORRIED
  that he might not.
- Jane feels a pain, and she's WORRIED she might
  be getting sick.
- People can also WORRY about other people: I'm
  WORRIED about Jim. He's not home yet.

What else can make someone feel WORRIED?

What makes *you* feel WORRIED?

RELIEVED: When someone has been WORRYING about something,
but it turns out OK

- Tom passed his spelling test, and he felt RELIEVED.
- Jane (the girl who had the pain who was WORRIED about
  getting sick) felt RELIEVED when _____.
- When Jim came home, we all felt _____.

What else can make someone feel RELIEVED?

What makes *you* feel RELIEVED?

# How Might Someone Feel? Part I

## PURPOSE

To strengthen children's awareness of ICPS feeling words, with focus on identifying the feeling associated with an event

## MATERIALS

Activity Sheet 1

Chalkboard or easel

People List (from Lesson 4)

Feeling Word List

## TEACHER SCRIPT

---

**NOTE**

You may find it useful to make a poster of the Feeling Word List given here for use in future lessons. Some teachers have also found it helpful to make or have children make a bulletin board display of all the ICPS feeling words, cut from colored construction paper. When the words are on display, children can see and choose the ones that fit their own and others' feelings when real problems come up.

---

*Give each child a copy of Activity Sheet 1. Write the People List and the Feeling Word List on the chalkboard (or refer children to previously prepared posters).*

### Feeling Word List

| | | | |
|---|---|---|---|
| 1. Happy | 5. Jealous | 9. Sympathetic | 13. Disappointed |
| 2. Angry | 6. Frustrated | 10. Ashamed | 14. Proud |
| 3. Sad | 7. Impatient | 11. Embarrassed | 15. Worried |
| 4. Afraid | 8. Lonely | 12. Surprised | 16. Relieved |

For today's ICPS game, we're going to use the People List and a new list, the Feeling Word List.

I'm going to tell you some things someone said.

You write in the *best* feeling word and the *one* person who might have said it.

*Direct children's attention to the People List and Feeling Word List for options, then use a dramatic voice and expression as you read the items on the activity sheet.*

*If desired, after the children have completed the exercise, they may read their answers to the group.*

1. Sammy won first prize in a contest. I never win anything.

   I feel _____ Who am I? _____

2. I'm sorry I said you stole my pencil. Now I know you didn't.

   I feel _____ Who am I? _____

3. You shouldn't have gone to Susan's house today. I asked you to clean your room.

   I feel _____ Who am I? _____

4. I was sitting in my house wishing my friends would come over to play, but they didn't.

   I feel _____ Who am I? _____

5. You promised me you'd throw out the trash. The trash is still there.

   I feel _____ Who am I? _____

6. Mark's dog died. Mark loved his dog.

   I feel _____ Who am I? _____

7. I told my friend a secret. I shouldn't have done that because he might tell somebody else.

   I feel _____ Who am I? _____

8. I thought she was going to get me a skateboard for my birthday. All she got me was a lousy old pair of socks.

   I feel _____ Who am I? _____

9. I was mad at him, so I spilled milk on his new clothes. Then I knew that was a stupid thing to do.

   I feel _____ Who am I? _____

10. I told you not to wander off when we were in the store. I thought you were lost. I couldn't find you.

    I feel _____ Who am I? _____

11. Oh, boy! A new dump truck.

    I feel _____ Who am I? _____

12. When you hit someone else in class, I don't like that.

    I feel _____ Who am I? _____

# ICPS Concepts: Same-Different, Two Things at the Same Time

### When a child is not listening:

Can you hear what I'm saying AND talk to your neighbor at the SAME TIME?

How do you think I feel when you talk at the SAME TIME I'm trying to explain something?

Can I hear _____ when everyone is talking at the SAME TIME?

Can I hear _____ better if everyone talks at the SAME TIME or at DIFFERENT times?

Everyone is listening to me. That makes me feel _____.

### When a child is off-task:

Can you work on your (math) and (daydream, talk to your neighbor) at the SAME TIME?

How will you feel if you don't get your work done on time?

### When a child is having trouble with homework:

When you bring in your homework and you did it all, how does that make you feel?

How do you feel when you do NOT finish your homework?

What were you doing when you should have been doing your homework?

Can you (talk on the telephone) and do your homework at the SAME TIME?

### When a child is trying hard:

I see you're really trying hard to solve that math problem, and I know you feel FRUSTRATED.

I'm PROUD of you for trying.

### When a child is attempting to solve a problem by using ICPS:

I see you're trying hard to solve that problem with _____, and I know you feel FRUSTRATED.

I bet if you think really hard, you can think of a DIFFERENT way.

# ICPS Feeling Words

*The following examples show how to integrate ICPS feeling words into math lessons. Ways of using them in other subject areas are presented following Lesson 25.*

Which would make you feel the most FRUSTRATED?
You are a runner and you just missed winning by:

a. $\frac{2}{5}$ of a minute

b. $\frac{1}{4}$ of an hour – 13 minutes

Which would make you feel the most IMPATIENT?
You had to wait for something you wanted for:

a. 15 days

b. 2 weeks + 2 days

c. 408 hours

Which would make you feel the most PROUD?
If you were learning to play basketball and
learned to shoot $4^2 + 2^3$ baskets per game in:

a. 3 years, 51 weeks

b. 3 years, 14 months

c. 3 years, 371 days

d. 4 years, 1 month

Which would make your family feel the most WORRIED?
You are late for dinner by:

a. 1 hour, 5 minutes, 70 seconds

b. 1 hour, 6 minutes, 3 seconds

c. 66 minutes, 4 seconds

Which would make you feel the most EMBARRASSED?
You overpaid a salesperson by:

a. 100 cents

b. 2 dollars – 150 cents

c. 50 cents + 60 cents

# Picture Concentration

## PURPOSE

To help children remember things about people, including their feelings and preferences

## MATERIALS

Illustrations 1–12

## TEACHER SCRIPT

---

### NOTE

Make two copies of each of the 12 illustrations provided. If desired, start with fewer pairs—increase the number according to your group's ability.

---

*To conduct this familiar game, follow these procedures:*

1. Give one illustration apiece to each of 24 game board participants. Have these children stay seated at their desks, keeping their illustrations facedown.

2. Ask the players (the remainder of the class) to stand up in front of the room.

3. Have the first player name a game board participant. This child turns his or her illustration over so all the players can see it.

4. Say, "Now, all you players remember who has the _____. The idea of this game is to find a match—another person who has the SAME picture." *(Describe the content of the illustration—for example, the boy on the skateboard.)*

5. Have the first player name another game board participant, who then turns his or her illustration over.

6. If there is no match: Instruct the two game board participants to turn their illustrations facedown. Invite a new player to try for a match by naming two more game board participants.

7. If there is a match: Instruct the two game board participants to leave their illustrations faceup on their desks. Invite a new player to try for a match by naming two more game board participants. (Having a new child guess, regardless of whether or not a match is made, means that more children can have a turn.)

8. Repeat with increasing numbers of game board participants and picture pairs as time and interest permit. Switch game board participants and players to allow more children to guess. Tally points if desired.

ILLUSTRATION 1  Lesson 16

ILLUSTRATION 2  Lesson 16

ILLUSTRATION 3   Lesson 16

ILLUSTRATION 4  Lesson 16

ILLUSTRATION 5   Lesson 16

ILLUSTRATION 6  Lesson 16

ILLUSTRATION 7   Lesson 16

ILLUSTRATION 8  Lesson 16

ILLUSTRATION 9   Lesson 16

ILLUSTRATION 10  Lesson 16

ILLUSTRATION 11  Lesson 16

ILLUSTRATION 12  Lesson 16

# Concentration Games

*Make index card sets with content like the following to help children further improve memory. Adapt the content to reflect what your own class is learning—let children make up their own examples. Tell children that this exercise is like the Picture Concentration Game except this time the match on the second card is an answer equal or related to that on the first card.*

## MATH

| Set 1 | Set 2 |
|---|---|
| $5 \times 5$ | $5^2$ |
| $\dfrac{18}{3}$ | 6 |
| XXIV | 24 |
| $\dfrac{6}{100}$ | .06 |
| $3^3$ | 27 |
| 24 months | 2 years |
| 4 quarts | 1 gallon |
| 3 feet | 1 yard |
| 9 | $\dfrac{3}{4}$ of 12 |
| 3 hours | 180 minutes |

## SCIENCE

| Set 1 | Set 2 |
|---|---|
| Camel | Lives in the desert |
| Paper clip | Can be magnetized |
| Battery | Energy source |

## SOCIAL STUDIES

**Set 1**

Thomas Jefferson

Martin Luther King

**Set 2**

Third President of the United States

Civil rights leader

## GEOGRAPHY

**Set 1**

Pennsylvania

Illinois

California

**Set 2**

Harrisburg

Springfield

Sacramento

# A Feeling Story

## PURPOSE

To encourage the use of previously learned ICPS feeling words
in sequenced thinking, for later planning of step-by-step means
to reach interpersonal goals

## MATERIALS

Chalkboard or easel

Feeling Word List (from Lesson 15)

## TEACHER SCRIPT

*Write the Feeling Word List on the chalkboard (or refer children to a previously prepared poster).*

For today's ICPS game, I'm going to start a story.

When I say the word *continuation,* raise your hand
if you want to continue the story.

The idea is to make up a story using DIFFERENT feeling
words. When it's your turn, try to continue the story, using
a feeling word.

You can use the SAME word someone else did, if you need
it in your story, but try to use a DIFFERENT word.

If you want to use a feeling word that is NOT on the board,
that's OK.

When you want someone else to go on with the story—or after
you use a feeling word—say the word *continuation.*

*Possible Story Starter:* Two kids were playing a game at recess, and
an older kid came and ruined the game. The
two kids felt _____.

*Say, "Continuation." You may have to use this word a few times until the group
catches on.*

## OPTIONS

1. Conduct the lesson with the whole class to give everyone the idea of the game. Write the story as it develops on the board, underlining the feeling words. Using the same or a different story beginning, repeat the game in small groups (possibly during reading time).

2. If competition is desired in the small-group format, tell each group to try to use more feeling words than the other groups. Have a recorder write the story on a piece of paper, rather than on the chalkboard, so the other groups cannot see it. Total the number of feeling words and record for each group.

3. Audiotape the story or stories for later playback. As children hear a feeling word, they can stand up or raise their hands.

4. If desired, let one child carry the entire story through, either on the same day as the lesson or on a later day.

5. Ask children to write their own stories, but only after the lesson has been conducted with the whole class and/or small groups. Otherwise, the class will not have the benefit of hearing others' ideas, and their repertoire of feeling words may be reduced.


## SAMPLE CONTINUATION STORY

*This story, given by a very competent 10-year-old, started with the idea that one child ruined some other children's game at recess.*

The boys felt *angry* 'cause the kid ruined their game. They felt *frustrated,* too, 'cause just at the best point of the game they couldn't get to the same place. The two kids punched the older kid, and the older kid got *mad.* They were *afraid* now 'cause he was *mad.* Then the gym teacher came up and said if they would be that way together, "You will have to be separated." So they were *lonely* 'cause they were separated, and they saw the bully going to play with his friend, and they were *jealous.* After school they were *worried* that the older boy would come back and get them back for punching him in the stomach 'cause he never did get them back. After school they were *surprised* he wasn't there. When he got home his mother had *sympathy* when he told her the story. He brought the other boy home to play with them. One of the boys said we were in a bad stage of the game anyhow—he just said that to make the other boy feel better. The other boy was *offended* because he was winning. So they broke up for a while. Then they started to *regret* what happened, and so they made up at school, and the older kid made up to them, and so they were all *happy.* The older boy was *embarrassed* that he had been so mean.

# Feeling Cartoons, Part I

## PURPOSE

To help children think further about what makes the SAME person feel DIFFERENT ways

## MATERIALS

Activity Sheets 2–5

## TEACHER SCRIPT

---

**NOTE**

You may give each of the four activity sheets to the entire class, or you may give those depicting boys to the boys in the class and those depicting girls to the girls. The activity sheets may also be used as a supplement at any time during the program when small groups are participating in other lessons.

---

*Give each child a copy of the activity sheets chosen.*

Are these pictures of the SAME child feeling DIFFERENT ways or DIFFERENT children feeling the SAME way?
*(Let children respond.)*

Above each picture are *cartoon balloons.*

In the comics (or funnies), these balloons are filled with words, words that people are thinking or saying.

*The following questions pertain to Activity Sheet 2. Adapt as necessary for the other sheets.*

OK. Let's say this is a girl your age.

In the first picture, the girl is feeling HAPPY. See the word HAPPY next to her picture?

You see there are five balloons above the girl who is feeling HAPPY.

In the HAPPY column, write in each balloon what the girl might be thinking about that would make her feel that way.

Write something DIFFERENT inside each balloon. You can just make it up.

When you finish with that, do the same thing for the next picture.

It is the SAME girl. How does she feel in this next picture?

Yes, WORRIED.

*Introduce another activity sheet, then ask children to fill in the cartoon balloons to show what the character might be thinking that would cause him or her to have the particular feeling.*

*Let some children read their cartoon balloons aloud and classify answers, pointing out enumerations. This can be done on the same day as the lesson or on a different day.*

*Common enumerations and guidelines for classifying them are as follows:*

HAPPY

*Receiving a present:* Birthday, Christmas

*Eating certain foods:* Ice cream, pizza

WORRIED

*Getting hurt:* Car accident, falling

*Someone is not home yet:* Mother, sister, brother

*Breaking something and getting in trouble:* Vase, toy

*Someone is lost:* Sister, brother, dog

*Something is lost:* Homework, toy

PROUD

*Schoolwork:* Good report card, passed test

*Winning something:* Race, prize, contest

FRUSTRATED

*Skill deficiency:* Sports, academics

*Breaking something:* Toy, shoelace

*Just missed something:* Bus, train, elevator

*Someone won't listen:* Watching television, reading, talking instead

AFRAID

*Being alone:* In the dark, at home

*Being followed:* In the street, in the attic, in a car

*Hearing a loud noise:* Firecracker, banging on wall

*Having someone sneak up on you:* Brother, sister, friend

DISAPPOINTED

*Not getting picked for something:* Club, play, team

*Not getting a good grade:* Spelling, math

*Not winning:* Game, contest

SURPRISED

*Receiving something:* Gift, surprise party, ticket

*Achieving something:* Good grades, trophy

IMPATIENT

*For something to be fixed:* Bike, television

*To get a turn:* To jump rope, to play a game or with a toy

*Whenever an enumeration appears, tell the class it is an enumeration because, for example:*

A brother and a sister sneaking up on you are enumerations because they both describe someone sneaking up on you.

Can you think of something DIFFERENT from someone sneaking up on you that would make you feel AFRAID?

Waiting for a bike to be fixed and waiting for a television to be fixed are enumerations because they're both waiting for something to be fixed.

Can you think of something DIFFERENT from waiting for something to be fixed that might make someone feel IMPATIENT?

## OPTIONS

1. After you have helped children classify enumerations, let pairs of children attempt to classify each other's enumerations. Pair more competent children with those having difficulty, and/or tell pairs of children to see if they had any of the same ideas. The children can then circle similar ideas. (Children enjoy doing this.)

2. Have children write their names on the backs of their completed activity sheets, then display them. The group can then look at them and pick out the enumerations. Some teachers like to make a bulletin board of all the children's responses.

**The SAME child can feel DIFFERENT ways**

HAPPY . . .

WORRIED . . .

# The SAME child can feel DIFFERENT ways

PROUD . . .

FRUSTRATED . . .

# The SAME child can feel DIFFERENT ways

AFRAID . . .

DISAPPOINTED . . .

# The SAME child can feel DIFFERENT ways

SURPRISED . . .

IMPATIENT . . .

# How Might Someone Feel? Part II

## PURPOSE

To strengthen children's awareness of ICPS feeling words, with focus on identifying the feeling associated with an event

## MATERIALS

Chalkboard or easel

Activity Sheet 6

People List (from Lesson 4)

Feeling Word List (from Lesson 15)

## TEACHER SCRIPT

*Give each child a copy of Activity Sheet 6. Write the Feeling Word List and the People List on the chalkboard (or refer children to previously prepared posters).*

Today I'm going to give you some more examples of what makes people feel the way they do.

You tell us the *best* feeling word and the *one* person who might have said it.

*Direct children's attention to the People List and the Feeling Word List for options, then use a dramatic voice and expression as you read the items on the activity sheet. If desired, after the children have completed the exercise, they may read their answers to the group.*

## OPTIONS

1. Ask if anyone can think of a feeling word on the list and give an example like the ones on the activity sheet.

2. Invite the group to make up their own examples, using feeling words.

3. Assign the activity sheet as homework. Have the children read their answers the next day.

1. Uh-oh! The truck won't start, and I can't get to work.

   I feel _____ Who am I? _____

2. I played basketball really well today. I scored the most points.

   I feel _____ Who am I? _____

3. When you won't let me play with your ball, and I let you play
   with my things, how do I feel?

   I feel _____ Who am I? _____

4. When you nag and pester me when you can't have what you want
   right away, how does that make me feel?

   I feel _____ Who am I? _____

5. Oh, you gave me a very nice present. I didn't know you were going
   to do that for me.

   I feel _____ Who am I? _____

6. I'm trying to tie five balloons together. Every time I almost finish,
   one of them pops.

   I feel _____ Who am I? _____

7. When I try to talk to you and you don't listen to me, how does that
   make me feel?

   I feel _____ Who am I? _____

8. Where's my new bike? My mom will really be mad if someone took it.
   She told me not to leave it outside.

   I feel _____ Who am I? _____

9. When I found my new bike, how did I feel then?

   I feel _____ Who am I? _____

10. Those kids are playing with the hydrant again. What if there isn't enough water
    when I need it?

    I feel _____ Who am I? _____

11. Why are you all laughing at me? Whoops! I made a mistake. I have on one red
    sock and one green sock.

    I feel _____ Who am I? _____

12. Mom, please, can I open my present now? Please, please! I can't wait.
    I want to open it right now.

    I feel _____ Who am I? _____

# How Can You Tell? Two Ways to Find Out

**PURPOSE**

To introduce the idea that there is more than one way to tell how someone feels

**MATERIALS**

Chalkboard or easel

Feeling Word List (from Lesson 15)

**TEACHER SCRIPT**

There's more than one way to tell if someone feels HAPPY.
Who can think of way number one?

*If there is no answer, or if the answer is "If the person laughs/smiles," point to your eyes and ask, "By _____?"*

That's *one* way. We can tell how someone feels by watching—by seeing how he or she looks.

Who can think of way number two? *(Point to your ears, if necessary.)*

Yes, we can tell by hearing (listening to) them.

Let's talk about telling how someone feels by watching.

*Mime HAPPY with a big smile, head lifted high, and brisk walk.*

How do I feel now?

Yes, I feel HAPPY.

How can you tell I feel HAPPY?

*If needed:* What is my mouth doing? Is my head up or down? How am I walking?

Now see if you can tell how I feel.

*Mime SAD with a frown, head down, and slow walk.*

If I'm looking like this, I'm probably NOT feeling _____.

Now I'm going to do two things to show you how I feel.

125

*Mime SAD by putting your head down and pretending to cry. (Make a crying sound.)*

How do I feel now?

Yes, SAD.

How could you tell? What's way number one?

Yes, you could tell by _____. *(Point to your eyes, if needed.)*

What's way number two? *(Point to your ears, if needed.)*

*If anyone says, "Ask" at this point, emphasize that you're looking for the two ways you already showed. Say, "Yes, you can ask. That's right. But what did I do to show you how I feel?"*

Now I'm going to *pantomime* some more feelings.

When we do what we call miming, we do NOT talk—we only use facial expressions or move our bodies.

*Demonstrate the following examples, using exaggerated movements and facial expressions. After each, ask the group what happened and what feeling you are expressing.*

FRUSTRATED: Trying to tie a shoelace that breaks, blowing up a balloon that pops

PROUD: Shooting baskets, making a hockey goal

WORRIED: Looking at your watch every 2 seconds

Now I need someone to pick a word from our Feeling Word List and mime that feeling.

You can show us any way you want to, but use only your body and your face—no words.

The rest of us will guess the feeling word you're miming.

*(After the performance, to the group)* If you think you can guess how _____ is feeling, raise your hand.

*(To the child who offers a guess)* What did _____ do that made you guess that one?

How can you find out if your guess is what _____ was showing?

*If the child who guessed does not ask the actor, let the group answer. Repeat with as many children as time and interest permit.*

---

**HINT**

If the group becomes noisy during this or any other lesson, ask, "How do I feel when you're noisy and we can't hear each other?" or "What can you do so we can have fun with this game and can hear each other?"

---

# How Can You Tell? A Third Way to Find Out

**PURPOSE**

To suggest yet another way children can find out how someone feels

**MATERIALS**

None

**TEACHER SCRIPT**

Now we have two ways to find out how people feel.

Way number one is watching *(point to your eyes)*, and way number two is _____. *(Point to your ears.)*

Who can think of way number three? *(If relevant:* Some of you did this at the end of the last lesson if you couldn't guess by watching.)

*If asking is not suggested as an answer:*

Listen to what I do.

(Child 1), what sport do you like? *(Let child respond.)*

What did I just do to find out?

Yes, I asked.

Now when (Child 1) told us, how did we know what (he/she) said? *(Point to your ears.)*

(Child 2), how can you find out what (Child 3's) favorite color is? *(If needed, point to your mouth.)*

Yes, you can ask. Go ahead and ask (him/her).

*Let children make up questions and practice asking.*

OK. Now raise your hand and tell about a time when you could tell that your mother or father was HAPPY just by:

- Watching
- Listening
- Asking
- Any two of these ways

*It may be helpful to point out that if you ask, you can hear what the person says; if someone is smiling, you can see but not hear; and if someone is laughing, you can see and hear.*

Now raise your hand and tell about a time when you could tell that your teacher was PROUD.

How could you tell?

Any other way?

What about a time when a classmate was ANGRY?

How could you tell?

Any other way?

What about a time when your teacher was FRUSTRATED?

How could you tell?

Any other way?

What about a time when your mother or father was WORRIED?

How could you tell?

Any other way?

What about a time when a friend was SAD?

How could you tell?

Any other way?

What about when a (brother/sister) was _____?

How could you tell?

Any other way?

*Invite the group to make up other examples.*

# How Can You Tell?

## FEELINGS AND PREFERENCES

### *When a child is (laughing, smiling, crying, or yelling):*

*(To other children)* How is _____ feeling?

How can you tell?

Yes, you can tell by (watching/listening).

How else can you tell?

### *When a child has an interpersonal problem:*

What happened? What's the matter?

Do (you two/ALL of you) see what happened the SAME way OR a DIFFERENT way?

How can you find out how _____ feel(s) about what happened?

### *When a child wants to play:*

You like to (play checkers).

Do you think _____ likes to (play checkers)?

How can you tell?

If you're not sure, how can you find out?

## MINI-DIALOGUE

**Situation:** Alice is sitting at her desk crying. Everyone in the class has gone to recess except for Karen.

Teacher: *(Out of Alice's earshot)* Karen, how does Alice feel?

Karen: Sad.

Teacher: How can you tell?

Karen: She's crying.

Teacher: Do you know why she's crying?

Karen: No.

Teacher: How can you find out?

Karen: I can ask her.

Teacher: Go ahead and ask her.

Karen:   *(To Alice)* What's wrong?

Alice:   I can't find my jump rope.

Teacher:   *(To Karen)* Can you think of a way to help Alice feel better?

Karen:   I can help her look for her jump rope.

*Notice how the teacher in this example encourages sensitivity toward another's feelings. Sometimes in a situation like this it might be better to guide the child to look for the lost article herself. However, encouraging another child to participate, as long as it does not embarrass the target child, does promote awareness and concern for others in distress.*

# How Could This Be?

## PURPOSE

To show that DIFFERENT people can feel DIFFERENT ways about the SAME thing

To help children begin to consider why people might feel the way they do

## MATERIALS

Chalkboard or easel

People List (from Lesson 4)

Feeling Word List (from Lesson 15)

## TEACHER SCRIPT

Today we're going to talk about how it could be that DIFFERENT people feel DIFFERENT ways about the SAME thing.

For example, Ruthie feels HAPPY when she sprays herself with water on a hot day.

*But* the fire fighter feels WORRIED that there won't be enough water to put out a fire.

Who else might NOT feel HAPPY that Ruthie uses water?

Johnny feels HAPPY when he stays out late.

*But* his mother feels WORRIED.

How could this be?

Why might these people feel the way they do? *(Let children respond.)*

Patty and her mother feel DIFFERENT ways when Patty's room is all messed up.

How could this be?

How does each person feel?

Why?

Tyrone and his father feel DIFFERENT ways when Tyrone's old model airplane breaks.

How could this be?

How does each person feel?

Why?

*Encourage children to make up situations in which someone says or does something that another person might feel differently about. Have them say how each person feels and why.*

OK, now we're going to change this game a little.

We just talked about something that *one* person does, or that happens to *one* person and how people can feel DIFFERENT ways about that.

Now we're going to talk about when *two* people are involved in the SAME thing, share the SAME experience, or own the SAME object.

You tell me why each person might feel a DIFFERENT way about something they're both involved in.

Jamie and Stacey were doing their arithmetic homework.

Jamie felt PROUD when she was doing hers.

Stacey felt FRUSTRATED.

How could this be?

Why might each person feel the way she does?

Ralph and Peter each got a basketball for their birthdays.

Ralph felt HAPPY about this.

Peter felt DISAPPOINTED.

How could this be?

Why might each person feel the way he does?

Janet is playing some really loud music, and she is HAPPY about it.

Her sister, Rachelle, is hearing that SAME music and feeling very ANGRY about it.

How could this be?

Why might each person feel the way she does?

Gary and Peter were asked to be in the school play.

They each felt a DIFFERENT way about doing this.

How might Gary have felt?

Why?

What DIFFERENT way might Peter have felt?

Why?

Sandra and Debbie both went on a roller-coaster ride.

They each felt a DIFFERENT way about doing this.

How might Sandra have felt?

Why?

How might Debbie have felt?

Why?

*Encourage children to think of additional examples that show how two people can feel a different way about the same situation.*

*Sometimes children's examples show that they are confused about the point of the lesson. If, for example, a child says, "JoAnne is happy because her hair is long, and Elizabeth feels jealous because her own hair is short," you could ask, "Could JoAnne and Elizabeth feel DIFFERENT ways if they both had long hair?"*

What did we learn from this lesson?
(*If needed:* DIFFERENT people may feel
DIFFERENT ways about the SAME thing.)

# How Do People Feel About Things?

## PURPOSE

To provide further practice in considering one's own and others' points of view

## MATERIALS

Chalkboard or easel

Activity Sheet 7

Feeling Word List (see Lesson 15)

## TEACHER SCRIPT

> **NOTE**
>
> This lesson may be written in class or given as homework.

*Write the Feeling Word List on the chalkboard (or refer children to a previously prepared poster).*

Today we're going to think about what makes us feel the way we do when someone does or says something.

*Give each child a copy of Activity Sheet 7. Have the group follow along as you discuss each part.*

This activity sheet is divided into five parts for you to think about.

Part 1 is what someone does or says that makes *you* feel the way you do.

That someone in the first part is your mother or whoever usually takes care of you.

Here you think about the way *you* look at things.

In Part 2, you'll think about how what you say or do makes your mother feel the way she does.

So here you'll think about how *she* looks at things.

In Part 3, the person will be a classmate.

In this part, you'll think of the SAME or a DIFFERENT classmate for the DIFFERENT feeling words.

First, you'll think about how your classmate makes *you* feel.

In Part 4, you'll think about how your classmate feels when you do or say something—how *he* or *she* might look at things.

If nothing like this usually happens to you, you can make these ideas up.

At the end of each of the first four parts is a blank where you can add any word from the Feeling Word List.

If you think of a word that's not on the list, it's OK to use it instead.

In Part 5, you fill in people from the People List and then say what these people do or say that makes you feel HAPPY, ANGRY, and so on.

You can use the SAME person for every item, or you can use DIFFERENT people.

*If the activity is done in class, you may want to repeat instructions for each part as children get to it.*

*When the entire exercise has been completed, invite children to read some of their answers to the group. Have children raise their hands if they wrote the same thing for any of the items.*

*If a seemingly inappropriate response is given, ask, "Why do you think that?" The child may have something relevant in mind.*

**Part 1:** My mother makes *me* feel . . .

1. HAPPY when she _____

2. ANGRY when she _____

3. SAD when she _____

4. DISAPPOINTED when she _____

5. _____ when she _____

**Part 2:** I make my *mother* feel . . .

1. HAPPY when I _____

2. ANGRY when I _____

3. SAD when I _____

4. DISAPPOINTED when I _____

5. _____ when I _____

**Part 3:** A classmate makes *me* feel . . .

1. HAPPY when _____

2. ANGRY when _____

3. SAD when _____

4. DISAPPOINTED when _____

5. _____ when _____

**Part 4:** I make a *classmate* feel . . .

1. HAPPY when I _____

2. ANGRY when I _____

3. SAD when I _____

4. DISAPPOINTED when I _____

5. _____ when I _____

**Part 5:** *I feel . . .*

*Fill in a person from the People List, then write what the person does that makes you feel ANGRY, FRUSTRATED, WORRIED, and RELIEVED.*

*Example*       I feel ANGRY when *my brother*
                   *takes my games without asking me.*

1. I feel ANGRY when _____

   _____

2. I feel FRUSTRATED when _____

   _____

3. I feel WORRIED when _____

   _____

4. I feel RELIEVED when _____

   _____

*Now fill in your own feeling words and something that makes you feel that way.*

*Example*       I feel *happy*
                 when *I eat pizza.*

1. I feel _____

   when _____

2. I feel _____

   when _____

# Do We Feel the Same Way About It?

## PURPOSE

To show that DIFFERENT people can feel DIFFERENT ways about the SAME thing

To stress that it is important to find things out to avoid false assumptions

## MATERIALS

Mini-Play 7

## TEACHER SCRIPT

---

**NOTE**

Make a copy of Mini-Play 7 for each actor, then circle each actor's part.

---

Today we have a mini-play about how asking can help us find things out about people.

*Pick two children to play the parts of Joseph and Ralph; play the part of the teacher yourself. When the actors finish reading the mini-play, ask the following questions:*

*(To the child playing Joseph)* What did you say to Ralph that made him think you didn't want to play with him?
*(If needed:* Did you tell him you didn't want to play checkers?*)*

*(To the child playing Ralph)* How could you have found out if Joseph just didn't want to play checkers?
*(If needed:* What could you have asked Joseph to find out if he didn't want to play checkers?*)*

What could you have done if you really wanted to play checkers instead of play with Joseph?

*(To the group)* In this mini-play, Ralph really wanted to play with Joseph.

What did you learn from this? *(If needed:* That DIFFERENT people can feel DIFFERENT ways about the _____ thing.*)*

If you want someone to do something, what do you have
to find out first?

Do you remember three ways to find out how someone feels?
*(If necessary, point to eyes, ears, mouth.)*

Do you remember what happened when Ralph asked Joseph
to play checkers?

What didn't Ralph find out about Joseph?

Can you remember a time when you wanted someone to
do something and he or she said no?

What can you find out next time that happens?

*Let two new children make up another mini-play in which one child has to find
out something about another by asking. Let them plan it for a few minutes in a
corner of the room or in the hallway before they act it out. Discuss.*

## CHECKERS

Ralph: Hi, Joseph. It's raining today, and we're going to have indoor recess. Let's play checkers.

Joseph: No! I don't want to.

Ralph: *(Walks away, looking sad.)*

Teacher: What's the matter, Ralph?

Ralph: Joseph doesn't want to play with me.

Teacher: How do you know that?

Ralph: He said no.

Teacher: Joseph, what did you say to Ralph?

Joseph: I said I didn't want to play checkers.

Ralph: No, you didn't. When I asked you to play, you said you didn't want to.

Teacher: Joseph, did you mean you didn't want to play checkers or that you didn't want to play with Ralph?

Joseph: I didn't want to play checkers.

Teacher: Ralph, do you want to play checkers or do you want to play with Joseph?

Ralph: I want to play with Joseph. I like checkers, so I thought he'd like that, too.

Teacher: Oh, you thought you both felt the SAME way about the SAME thing. But you feel DIFFERENT ways, right?

Ralph: Right.

Teacher: How can you find out what you both feel the SAME way about? Something that would make both of you feel HAPPY?

Ralph: *(To Joseph)* Do you like to draw?

Joseph: No, I'm not good at that.

Ralph: Do you like to play tag?

Joseph: No, that's no fun.

*Finish this mini-play in your own way.*

# Do You Remember? Part II

## PURPOSE

To provide additional practice in paying attention and remembering, this time with a focus on feelings

## MATERIALS

None

## TEACHER SCRIPT

*Divide the class into two groups, each with panel members and players, and follow the procedures described in Lesson 13. This time, however, children who were panel members are now players, and vice versa. Tally correct answers, making sure each team has an equal number of questions.*

> Today we're going to play the Do You Remember Game again, but this time it's going to be harder.
>
> I'm going to ask two things of each panel member, and the players have to remember both things to get a point.
>
> *(To each of the Team A panel members)* _____, tell us what makes you feel PROUD and what makes you feel AFRAID.

*Record children's names and their responses for each feeling, or have a child record this information.*

> *(To Team A players)* Who can tell us what each Team A panel member said makes him or her feel PROUD and AFRAID?
>
> You have to remember both for your team to get the point.

*You may ask about each panel member's responses in any order. However, the idea is to find out what makes one panel member proud and afraid before going on to the next. If a player remembers one response, another player on the team can recall the other for the point. Tally points as they are earned.*

> *(To Team B panel members)* Each of you tell us what makes you feel HAPPY and what makes you feel DISAPPOINTED.

*Record children's names and their responses for each feeling, or have a child record this information.*

*(To Team B players)* Who can tell us what each Team B panel member said makes him or her feel HAPPY and what makes him or her feel DISAPPOINTED?

You have to remember both for your team to get the point.

*As for Team A, a second player can get the point if the first can remember only one response. Elicit both responses before asking about another panel member's responses. Tally points as they are earned.*

*(To Team A panel members)* Here's round two.

Each of you tell us again what makes you feel PROUD and what makes you feel AFRAID.

*Refer to the record sheet to ensure that children give the same responses they did earlier.*

Now tell us something someone in your grade could do to make someone else feel ANGRY.

*Record these responses on the same sheet used earlier.*

*(To Team A players)* Who can remember all three things the Team A panel members said?

What makes each one feel PROUD and AFRAID?

What do they think would make someone else ANGRY?

*Next ask the following questions, tallying each correct answer.*

Who said _____ makes him or her feel PROUD?
*(Repeat a response.)*

Who said _____ makes him or her feel AFRAID?
*(Repeat another response.)*

What did (Child 1) say makes (him/her) feel PROUD?

What did (Child 2) say someone in your grade could do to make someone else feel ANGRY?

*Continue asking these types of questions until Team A players start missing.*

*(To Team B panel members)* Each of you tell us again what makes you feel HAPPY and what makes you feel DISAPPOINTED.

*Refer to the record sheet to ensure that children give the same responses they did earlier.*

> Now tell us something someone in your grade could do to make someone else feel SURPRISED.

*Record these responses on the same sheet used earlier.*

> (*To Team B players*) Who can remember all three things the Team B panel members said?
>
> What makes each one feel HAPPY and DISAPPOINTED?
>
> What do they think would make someone else feel SURPRISED?

*Ask the following questions, tallying each correct answer.*

> Who said _____ makes him or her feel HAPPY?
> (*Repeat a response.*)
>
> Who said _____ makes him or her feel DISAPPOINTED?
> (*Repeat another response.*)
>
> What did (Child 1) say makes (him/her) feel HAPPY?
>
> What did (Child 2) say someone in your grade could do to make someone else feel SURPRISED?

*Ask the same number of questions as you did of the Team A players, compare final scores, then ask the following questions:*

> Why is it important to remember things about people?
>
> Do you remember the mini-play about Ralph, who thought Joseph didn't want to play with him? (*See Lesson 24.*)
>
> How could remembering things about Joseph have helped Ralph?

# More ICPS Feeling Words

*List all the ICPS feeling words on chalkboard or easel, or use a previously prepared poster (see Lesson 15). Refer children to the list as needed.*

## READING AND STORY COMPREHENSION

In the story we just read, how do you think _____ felt
when _____?
*(Name a character and describe an event from the story.)*

Why do you think (he/she) felt that way?

Do you think any two characters felt the SAME way about
the SAME thing?

Do you think anyone felt a DIFFERENT way from
_____ about that?

## SOCIAL STUDIES

What made Alexander Graham Bell feel PROUD?

Marie Curie?

Neil Armstrong?

Frederick Douglass?

Babe Ruth?

*Let the class think of others.*

Think of (three, four, or five) DIFFERENT ways the following
people might feel, and why.

- Police officer
- Mayor of a city
- Astronaut
- Father
- Teacher
- Doctor

How might people from DIFFERENT cultures feel DIFFERENT ways about any of the following? *(Name specific cultures studied.)*

- Food
- Art
- Music
- Religion

## SCIENCE AND HEALTH

How do you feel about the following?

- Air pollution
- Drug/alcohol abuse
- Water pollution
- Smoking cigarettes
- The ozone layer
- Noise pollution

## GEOGRAPHY

Would a skier be happier in New York City OR in Switzerland?
Would a sunbather be happier in Alaska OR in Florida?

# How Can You Tell?

## READING AND STORY COMPREHENSION

How do you think _____ felt about _____?
*(Name a character and describe an event from the story.)*

How could you tell? (*If needed:* What did he or she say? How did he or she look?)

Did anyone in the story find out something about someone else by asking?

## MATH

Pamela had 25 nickels. Beth had 14 dimes plus 5 pennies.

Pamela felt HAPPY, but Beth felt SAD.

How could this be?

(*Possible answer:* Pamela had enough money to buy what she wanted, but Beth needed more.)

## SCIENCE

How many ways can you tell:

- A train is coming
- Someone is making popcorn

*Let children think of more examples.*

How can you find out:

- The optimum temperature range of water for germinating beans
- What organisms are near your school
- The optimum amount of water for a plant
- The optimum temperature for fish in an aquarium
- The optimum amount of fertilizer for growing plants

*If the answer is by watching (seeing, observing), ask, "How can you observe these things?" In the case of the optimum amount of water for a plant, for example, you might elicit the idea of conducting an experiment in which different plants receive different amounts of water.*

# How Do They Feel? What Do They Think?

## PURPOSE

To show children that there may be more than one—in this case, more than one motive for someone's behavior, more than one way someone feels about what another person does, and more than one way someone might think about what another person does

## MATERIALS

Illustrations 13–18

Activity Sheets 8–13

## TEACHER SCRIPT

Today we're going to talk more about why people might do the things they do and how other people might feel when they do it.

We're also going to talk about something new—what people think about when someone does something.

Let's start with this: Suppose Tommy sneaks in front of Ralph in line.

Why might Tommy do that?

Raise your hand if you can tell us.

*(To the child who responds)* How might (for example, wanting to be first) make Tommy want to sneak in front of Ralph like that? *(Let the same child respond.)*

*(To the group)* Raise your hand if you can think of a DIFFERENT reason Tommy might have done that. *(Let children respond.)*

How might that make him want to sneak in line?

*Ask a few more children to describe different reasons Tommy might have sneaked in front of Ralph.*

How do you think Ralph might feel when Tommy sneaks in front of him? *(Let children respond.)*

Is there any other way Ralph might feel?

What might Ralph be thinking?

Now we're going to break up into groups.

I've got some pictures, and I'm going to give a picture to each group.

*Divide the class into six groups. Give each group one illustration and a copy of the activity sheet corresponding to it.*

*Try to include some verbal and some less verbal youngsters in each group. Have one child in each group read the questions to the rest of the group.*

*(To each group)* Look at your picture and think about the questions you have about it.

You can have 5 minutes to talk about the questions in your group, then each group will tell the class what they decided.

I'm going to ask each one of you to give the answer to a question.

*Visit each group as they discuss to make sure they understand the questions.*

*After they have finished discussing the questions, have them present their decisions to the group. Encourage every child to report an answer. If more than five children are in a group, let them give a different answer to any question.*

*After each group gives their presentation, encourage the rest of the class to add any thoughts they may have to the discussion.*

*If you run out of time before all the groups have presented their decisions, record the names of the children in each group. You may tell any groups that did not present their decisions that they will have their turn another time.*

ILLUSTRATION 13  Lesson 26

ILLUSTRATION 14  Lesson 26

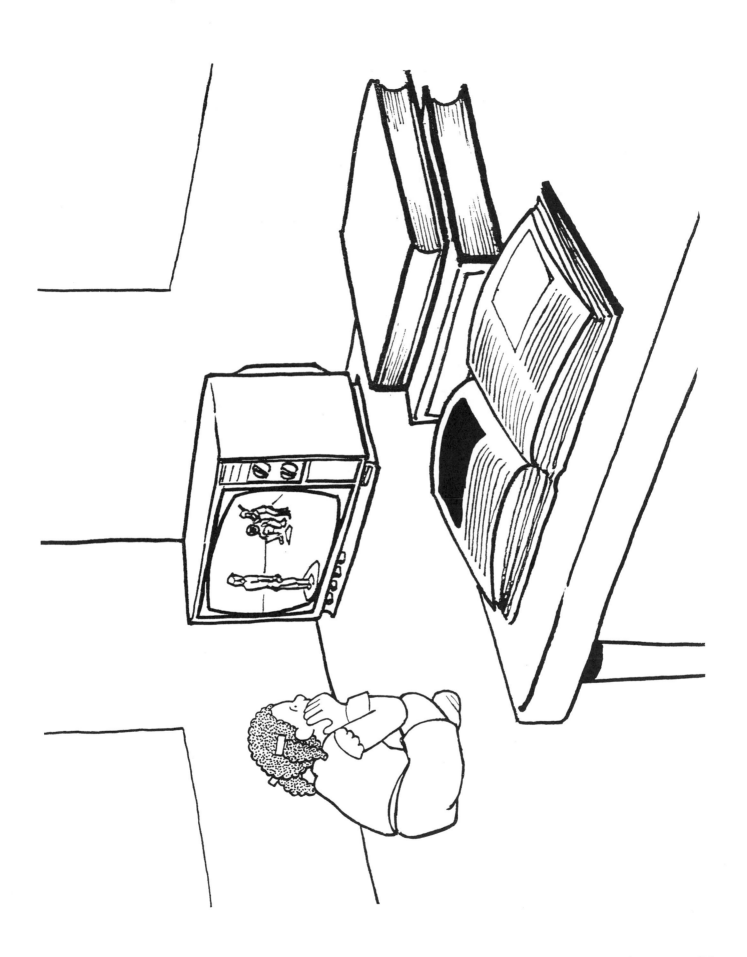

ILLUSTRATION 15    Lesson 26

ILLUSTRATION 16  Lesson 26

ILLUSTRATION 17   Lesson 26

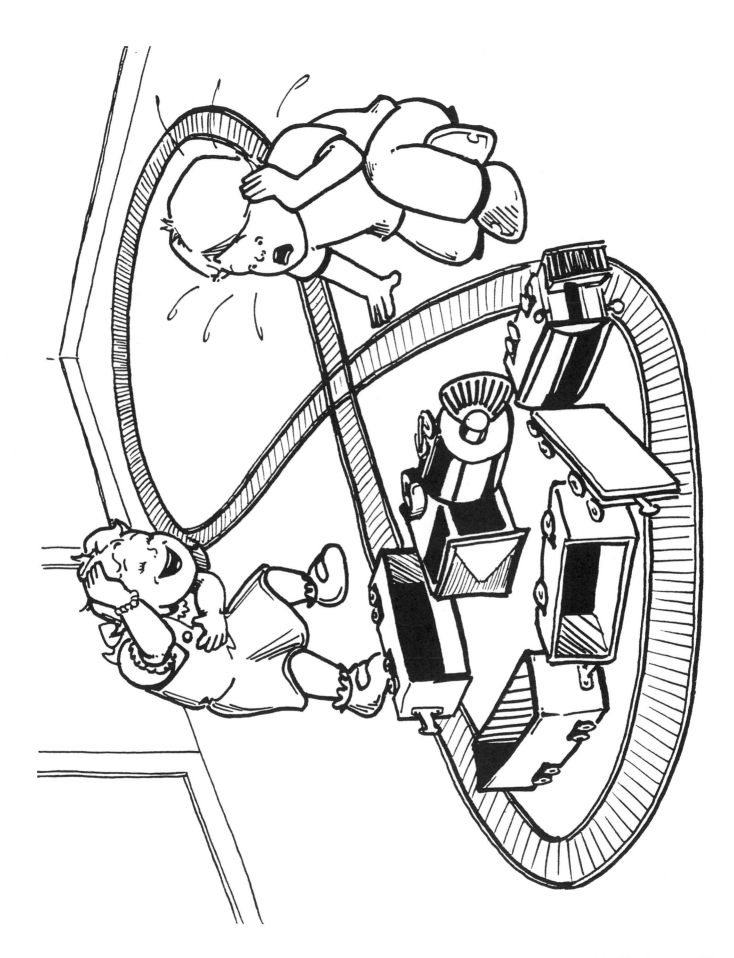

ILLUSTRATION 18  Lesson 26

**GROUP 1: ILLUSTRATION 13**

This boy tells his friends that he is a yo-yo champ when he is not.

1. Why might this boy tell his friends that he is a yo-yo champ when he is not?

2. How might he *feel* when he tells his friends he is a yo-yo champ when he really isn't?

3. Is there any other way he might *feel*?

4. If his friends find out he is not a yo-yo champ, how might they *feel*?

5. What might his friends *think* to themselves if they find out the boy is not really a yo-yo champ?

ACTIVITY SHEET 8   Lesson 26

This boy brags about how fast he can run.

1. Why might somcone brag about how fast he can run?

2. How might this boy *feel* when he brags like that?

3. Is there any other way he might *feel?*

4. How might this boy's friend *feel* when this boy is bragging about how fast he can run?

5. What might this boy's friend *think* to himself when the boy is bragging?

**GROUP 3: ILLUSTRATION 15**

This girl has not returned the books she borrowed.

1. Why might someone not return books she borrowed?

2. How might a person *feel* about doing that?

3. Is there any other way a person who does that might *feel*?

4. How might the person she borrowed the books from *feel* about not getting the books back?

5. What might the other person *think* about this girl when she does not return the books?

## GROUP 4: ILLUSTRATION 16

This boy has borrowed some money that he has no intention of giving back.

1. Why might someone borrow money and then not give it back?

2. How might this boy *feel* when he does that?

3. Is there any other way he might *feel?*

4. How might the person the boy borrowed the money from *feel* when he does not get his money back?

5. What might the person who does not get his money back *think* to himself?

**GROUP 5: ILLUSTRATION 17**

This girl is teasing her neighbor.

1. Why might this girl want to tease her neighbor?

2. How might she *feel* when she teases her neighbor?

3. Is there any other way she might *feel?*

4. How might the neighbor *feel* when she is teased like that?

5. What might her neighbor *think* to herself when she is teased like that?

This girl is laughing at her friend because her friend's train set broke.

1. Why might someone laugh at a friend when the friend is sad about something, like a broken train set?

2. How might the girl *feel* when she laughs at her friend like that?

3. Is there any other way she might *feel?*

4. How might the boy whose train set broke *feel* when the girl laughs?

5. When his friend laughs at him, what might the boy whose train set broke *think* to himself?

# Role-Playing, Part I

## PURPOSE

To help children experience the sensation of being on different ends of a problem situation, in order to further develop perspective taking and to encourage appreciation of why people might act the way they do

## MATERIALS

Chalkboard or easel

## TEACHER SCRIPT

**NOTE**

Parts 1 and 2 may be conducted in one session or, if time does not permit, at two separate times.

### Part 1

Today we're going to do what we call *role-playing.*

Role-playing is acting out a scene, making up what someone says and does.

Remember the game when I said, "I told you not to wander off when we were in the store. I thought you were lost. I couldn't find you"?

When I said that, I was pretending I was someone's mother.

Now I'm going to pretend I'm someone else.

See if you can guess who I'm pretending to be.

*Take the role of someone with whom all the children are familiar. For example:*

OK, I'm going to take your temperature now.

Hmmm! It looks like you have a fever.

Uh-oh, it looks like your throat is a little red, too.

Who am I pretending to be?

That's right, a doctor.

*Next pick a generally verbal child to help you demonstrate role-playing with two characters.*

(*To the group*) I'm going to pretend to be a sales clerk trying to sell (Child 1) a shirt that (he/she) doesn't want to buy.

(Child 1), come up and be the customer who doesn't like the shirt.

| | |
|---|---|
| Teacher: | (*As sales clerk*) Hello. That's a lovely shirt you're looking at. Those purple stripes and green polka dots will go great with your red-checked pants. And it's just your size. (*Hold hands up, exaggerating size.*) You do like it, don't you? |
| Child: | (*Responds.*) |
| Teacher: | Don't you think it goes with your shoes? |
| Child: | (*Responds.*) |
| Teacher: | What's your size? |
| Child: | (*Responds.*) |
| Teacher: | OK. What shirt do you want? |

*Ad lib as time and interest permit, then switch roles. Ask the child to pretend to sell you something different.*

(*To the group*) (Child 1) and I played both parts.

We each pretended to be two people.

First I was the sales clerk and (Child 1) was the customer, then we switched parts.

Now we're going to play some roles that *really* happen.

You've all heard people brag about something, or tease or pester someone.

We're going to play some of these roles.

Remember when we talked about how people might feel when someone brags to them about something?

Who wants to come up and play the part of a bragger? (*Choose a volunteer.*)

Now we need someone this child is going to brag to. (*Choose a child who will not be upset by the scenario.*)

(*To Child 2, the bragger*) What will you say to (Child 3)?

(*To Child 3*) How do you feel and what will you say? (*If needed:* How can you find out why Child 2 is bragging like that?)

*Encourage the two actors to continue the role-play as long as time and interest permit.*

> *(To the group)* How could you tell (Child 2) was bragging?
>
> *(Point to your eyes.)* What could you see (him/her) doing that would tell you (he/she) was bragging?
>
> How else could you tell (he/she) was bragging?
>
> *(Point to your ears.)* What did you hear?
>
> *(To the same two children)* OK, now switch parts.
> *(To Child 2)* You be the one being bragged to.
>
> *(To Child 3)* And you be the bragger now.
>
> Play the parts a DIFFERENT way. I mean, think about something DIFFERENT to brag about.

*Let children in the class comment briefly on the role-play after it is complete.*

## Part 2

> Now I'm going to write on the chalkboard some pairs of people to role-play. When you see a part you'd like to play, raise your hand and we'll find you a partner.

*Write the following pairs on the chalkboard.*

| | |
|---|---|
| Bossy person | Person being bossed |
| Person grabbing | Person being grabbed from |
| Teaser | Person being teased |
| Mother | Nagging child |
| Pest | Person being pestered |

*Help children role-play the situations they choose. After the first situation has been role-played, ask the following questions:*

> *(To the group)* Why do you think we are playing this game?
> *(If needed:* Why is it important to know how another person feels?)
>
> Why do you think a person might (for example, boss you)?
>
> Can you think of another reason?

What might you do or say if _____ is why you think that person might be (bossing you)? *(Repeat the first reason.)*

What might you do or say if _____ is why you think that person might be (bossing you)? *(Repeat the second reason.)*

OK, if a person (bosses you), is it possible that you might do or say something DIFFERENT if you think about why he or she is doing that?

*Repeat these questions for at least one of the other role-plays.*

# Three-Person Problems

## PURPOSE

To expand perspective taking to include three people, a precursor to more complex problem solving and consequential thinking

## MATERIALS

None

## TEACHER SCRIPT

Now let's talk about how people think and feel when three of them are having a problem.

I'm going to tell you the problem and then ask you to think about some questions.

The problem is that Betty and Larry's mother baked a special cake she was saving for dinner that night.

Betty and Larry saw the cake in the afternoon, and Larry said, "Betty, let's eat a piece of that cake now! I can't wait till later!"

How might Betty feel about doing this?

Why might Betty feel _____?
*(Repeat response—for example, afraid.)*

How might Larry feel about doing this?

Why might Larry feel that way?

Is Larry thinking about how their mother might feel when she finds out they ate some of the cake in the afternoon?

*If yes:* How does he think their mother might feel? Why?

*If no:* If Larry *did* think about it, how might he think she'd feel? Why?

Is Betty thinking about how their mother might feel when she finds out about this?

*If yes:* How does she think their mother might feel? Why?

*If no:* If she *did* think about it, how would she think their mother might feel? Why?

Can you think of a problem that came up between three kids or two kids and a (parent/teacher)?

*Let children describe a problem. Ask them how they think each of the three people felt about what happened and whether they felt the same way or different ways about the situation. Discuss as many three-person problems as time and interest permit.*

# Why Else Might That Have Happened?

## PURPOSE

To illustrate that there is more than one reason people do what they do, in order to help children later recognize what the problem is in specific situations

## MATERIALS

None

## TEACHER SCRIPT

Today we're going to talk about how things are not always what they seem to be.

There's often more than one reason for things.

We're going to play the Why Else Might That Have Happened Game?

Sometimes we get upset with people too soon, before we really know why they did or said something.

I'm going to tell you some situations when someone did or said something, but it could be for DIFFERENT reasons.

See if you can figure out what some of these reasons might be.

**Situation 1:** Jim is sitting on a bench, and Paul walks by and waves to him. Jim does not wave back. Paul thinks Jim is ANGRY at him.

Why else might Jim not have waved back to Paul?

How might Paul feel if _____? (*Repeat child's answer.*
*For example:* Jim had something else on his mind.)

Is there any other reason Jim might not have waved to Paul?

How might Paul feel if _____? (*For example:* Jim didn't see him.)

Would Paul feel a DIFFERENT way if he thought Jim really was ANGRY at him than he would if he thought _____?
(*For example:* Jim had something else on his mind,
Jim didn't see him.)

Is it a good idea to find out why someone did something before feeling _____? (*For example:* Hurt, angry)?

**Situation 2:** Randi asks Carolyn if her mother is coming to see her in the school play. Carolyn gets upset and walks away. Randi thinks Carolyn is ANGRY with her.

*Repeat the line of questioning given for Situation 1 for this and all subsequent situations.*

**Situation 3:** Tom stomps in the house and slams the door. His mother thinks he's doing that just to annoy her.

**Situation 4:** Marian told Denise that she couldn't go to the movies with her after school today. Denise thinks Marian doesn't want to be her friend anymore.

**Situation 5:** Benjamin isn't listening to the teacher today. The teacher thinks Benjamin doesn't care about the lesson.

Can you think of another example of something that someone might do or say for which there could be more than one reason?

You can think of something that really happened, or you can make it up.

---

**HINT**

If Activity Sheets 2–5 from Lesson 18 are incomplete, you may wish to have children finish them at this point.

---

# Things Are Not Always What They Seem

**When a child accidentally bumped from behind impulsively strikes the child who did the bumping:**

Do you remember the game we called Why Else Might That Have Happened?

There's often more than one reason for things.

Why do you think you got bumped by _____?
(*If appropriate:* Why else might that have happened?)

Is it a good idea to find out why someone did something before getting ANGRY?

How can you find out?

*Sometimes a child is more angry that another child did not say, "Excuse me" than he or she is about being bumped into. It can often change the mood if you say:*

I know that makes you ANGRY.

Hitting is *one* way to show _____ how you feel.

Can you think of a DIFFERENT way to show how you feel?

**When a child pushes in line:**

(*To the group*) Why do people push in line?

Why else?

Can anybody think of a still DIFFERENT reason?

(*To the child who was pushed*) What was your reason?

How might the person you pushed feel about that?

What might that person think to (himself/herself)?

What else could you do or say so _____?
(*Repeat reason or goal.*)

# Let Me Tell You Why

## PURPOSE

To suggest the importance of finding out why things happen before venting emotions

## MATERIALS

Mini-Play 8

## TEACHER SCRIPT

> **NOTE**
>
> Make a copy of Mini-Play 8 for each actor, then circle each actor's part.

Today we're going to have another mini-play.

This mini-play is about one person's getting ANGRY at another before finding out what really happened.

I want those of you in the audience to listen carefully because I'm going to ask some questions at the end.

*Select two children to take the parts of Ted and Kerry. After the children have acted out the mini-play, ask the following questions:*

How did Ted feel before he found out why Kerry didn't bring his basketball back?

Any other way?

How did Kerry feel when Ted wouldn't listen to him?

What might Ted have asked before getting _____?
*(Repeat stated feelings.)*

Why else might Kerry not have brought back Ted's basketball?

## THE BASKETBALL PROBLEM

Ted:   Kerry, you promised me you'd bring back my basketball today, and you didn't.

Kerry:   I couldn't bring it today. I . . .

Ted:   *(Interrupting)* I'll never let you use anything of mine again!

Kerry:   If you'd listen to me, I can tell you why.

Ted:   OK. Tell me.

Kerry:   I had to take my baby brother to the doctor. Mom was at work, and he fell and broke his arm. I couldn't carry your basketball and my baby brother. Then Mom came, took him to the hospital, and I came right to school.

Ted:   Oh.

# What Do They Know?

## PURPOSE

To extend perspective taking to thinking about simultaneous coordination of more than one viewpoint, based on differential knowledge about a situation

## MATERIALS

Chalkboard or easel

Name tags

A "present" (any appropriate prop)

Wrapping paper and tape

## TEACHER SCRIPT

> **NOTE**
> Before beginning, make three name tags, reading *Tara, Rachel,* and *Paulette.*

*Choose three girls. Give each one of them a name tag.*

Today we're going to role-play again.

That means to act out a scene, making up what someone says and does.

Let's call this one "The Birthday Present."

These girls are going to play Tara, Paulette, and Rachel.

*(To the girls)* Let's pretend you three are sisters.

Paulette, today's your birthday, and Tara's going to give you a present.

Let's imagine that Rachel gave you a present yesterday.

OK, now you three go out in the hall and wait until I call you in.

*(To the group)* Here's the story.

Tara wraps Paulette's birthday present really nicely and leaves it for Paulette to find—you know, a surprise.

Tara then leaves the house.

Meanwhile, Rachel comes in, sees the present, and opens it because she's IMPATIENT—you know, she can't wait to see what's inside.

Rachel leaves the open present in the house and goes out.

Later, Paulette sees the box, all opened.

She knows it was her present, but before she even sees what it is, she sits down in front of it and just about cries.

She feels very SAD.

Just then, Tara comes in and sees Paulette looking very SAD. Remember, Tara wrapped the present.

Why does she think Paulette is so SAD?

*If a child says, "Because Rachel opened it":* What else might she think? Remember, Tara did NOT know Rachel opened the present.

*If a child says Tara thinks Paulette does not like her present or gives another relevant reason:* Yes, that could be what she thinks.

OK, now the players are going to act out this story. Don't tell them what we know. It's our secret, OK?

*Call in the child playing Tara.*

Tara, you wrap this present nicely and then leave it on the floor (or table).

When you are finished, go back out in the hall, but don't tell the others what you did.

*Call in the child playing Rachel.*

This is your sister's birthday present.

Let's pretend you're IMPATIENT to see it, so you open it now. When you're finished, go back to your seat in the classroom.

*Call in the child playing Paulette.*

Today's your birthday, and this is your present from your sister Tara.

Oh, look, it's already opened.

Show us how you would feel if somebody opened *your* present.

OK, Paulette, sit down next to the present, look at it and keep looking SAD, like you're just about to cry.

*Call in the child playing Tara.*

Tara, why do you think Paulette is looking so SAD?

*(If Tara says Paulette does not like her present or gives any reason other than that Rachel opened it: Can you think of any other reason?)*

*Draw the following stick figures on the chalkboard. Point to these drawings as necessary.*

TARA
WRAPPED PRESENT

RACHEL
OPENED IT

PAULETTE'S
BIRTHDAY PRESENT

*(To the group)* Why is Paulette really SAD?

Why does Tara think Paulette is SAD?

What does Rachel know about why Paulette is SAD that Tara does NOT know?

Would it be a good idea for Tara to find out why Paulette is SAD before thinking that Paulette doesn't like her present?

Is there anything else anyone would like to say about this story?

Now let's change this situation a little.

If Tara knew Rachel opened the present because she was IMPATIENT, how would Tara feel?

Would Tara feel the SAME way or a DIFFERENT way if she found out Rachel opened it because she thought the present was really for her?

Why would she feel that way?

# More What Do They Know?

## PURPOSE

To further emphasize the need to avoid false conclusions

## MATERIALS

Mini-Play 9

Chalkboard or easel

## TEACHER SCRIPT

> **NOTE**
> Make a copy of Mini-Play 9 for each actor, then circle each actor's part.

Today we need three actors.

Listen carefully as they read their parts because I'll ask you some questions when they're finished.

*Give the children playing Sherry and Dawn their scripts. Tell the child playing Annette to draw a picture of anything she wants on the chalkboard, then leave the room.*

*Stop the players and call Annette back into the room after Sherry says, "It's too big for you, but it will only drag on the floor a little bit." Have them continue with the play.*

*When finished, ask the following questions:*

*(To the group)* What did Annette think Sherry was talking about?

What did Sherry think Annette worked so hard on?

What did Sherry mean when she said, "It's really ugly?" What was the "it"?

How did Annette feel before she found out what Sherry was really talking about?

What could Annette have asked Sherry before she thought Sherry was talking about her picture?

*(To the child playing Annette)* How do you feel now that you know Sherry wasn't talking about your picture?

## THE DRAWING

Annette:   *(Draws a picture on the chalkboard, then leaves.)*

Dawn:   *(To Sherry)* Hi, Sherry. I made something for you.
I think you'll like it. It's a purple dress with blue stripes
and yellow polka dots. It's too big for you, but it will only
drag on the floor a little bit.

Annette:   *(Reenters.)*

Sherry:   No, Dawn, I don't like it.

Dawn:   You don't like it?

Annette:   I heard you, Sherry. I worked very hard
on this. You never like anything I do.

Sherry:   Well, Dawn, it's really ugly.

Annette:   Well, I bet you can't make a better one.

Sherry:   I bet I can.

# Did That Really Happen?

## PURPOSE

To illustrate that avoiding false assumptions extends beyond why people do things to causes of events

## MATERIALS

Mini-Play 10

Any two hand puppets (optional)

## TEACHER SCRIPT

> **NOTE**
>
> Make a copy of Mini-Play 10 for each actor, then circle each actor's part.

The other day we talked about why *people* do things, like when one child does not wave to another or when one child gets upset when someone asks her if her mother is coming to the school play.

We discovered there are lots of possible reasons people do what they do.

Things are not always what they seem to be.

We also need to think about why *things* happen—like why a sweater might be missing from your closet.

Again, things are not always what they seem to be.

We might think someone took that sweater.

Maybe someone did, and maybe someone did NOT.

Have you ever heard this kind of thing?

*Change voices for the following two people; use puppets if desired.*

Person A says, "You took my sweater! Give it back!"

Person B says, "But I didn't take it!"

Person A insists, "Yes, you did!"

Who can think of something DIFFERENT that might have happened to the sweater?

*Elicit as many ideas as possible.*

How might Person A feel when he first thinks someone else has taken the sweater?

Person B knows she didn't take it. How might Person B feel when Person A insists she did?

How might Person A feel when he finds out Person B really didn't take it?

What else could Person A have done or said before telling Person B he thinks she took the sweater?

*Elicit as many ideas as possible.*

OK, now I'm going to change the story a little.

Marge and Nancy are talking to each other.

Tammy thinks they are saying nasty things about her, but they're really not.

Tammy goes up to them and hits them, then all three of them start fighting.

Do Marge and Nancy even know why Tammy hit them?

How might Marge and Nancy feel when Tammy hits them?

How might Tammy feel when she finds out they really didn't say nasty things about her?

What could Tammy have done before she hit the other two kids?

*Elicit as many ideas as possible, then choose two children to act out Mini-Play 10. After the mini-play, ask the following questions:*

*(To the child playing John)* What else might have happened to the pencil?

*(To the child playing Peter)* How did you feel when John said you took his pencil?

*(To the child playing John)* How would you feel if you found out Peter really didn't take your pencil?

What else could you have done or said before telling Peter you thought he took your pencil?

*Ask the group for additional ideas about what John could have done or said. Then have the two actors perform the scene again, this time so John finds out Peter really didn't take his pencil.*

## THE PENCIL

John:   Peter, I'm really mad. You took my pencil!

Peter:   Now *I'm* mad. I didn't take it!

John:   Yes, you did, 'cause I have a yellow pencil with a big eraser.

Pctcr:   But my brother gave me this pencil this morning.

John:   No, he didn't. That's my pencil, and I want it back!

# More Things Are Not Always What They Seem

### MINI-DIALOGUE

**Situation:** One child accuses another of stealing his pencil without gathering information first.

Teacher: Tommy, what can you do before telling Karl you think he took your pencil?

Tommy: I know he took it. He always steals my things.

Teacher: Are you sure he took it this time?

Tommy: I looked in my desk and on the floor.

Teacher: Think of all the places you've been today.

Tommy: In my locker . . . in the gym . . . and on the playground.

Teacher: What can you do next?

Tommy: Look in those places.

Teacher: Go ahead and look at recess time.

*After recess . . .*

Tommy: I didn't find it.

Teacher: What else might have happened to it? Think hard.

Tommy: Maybe I left it at home.

*The next day . . .*

Tommy: I found my pencil at home.

Teacher: Good. How do you think Karl felt yesterday when you got mad at him for taking your pencil?

Tommy: Mad.

Teacher: How do you feel now about accusing him?

Tommy: Embarrassed.

*If you have reason to believe a child did in fact take something without permission, see the ICPS dialogue involving Shawn and Lamont, following Lesson 48.*

# What's the Problem?

## PURPOSE

To emphasize that DIFFERENT people can see the SAME thing in DIFFERENT ways

## MATERIALS

Illustration 19

## TEACHER SCRIPT

I'm going to show you a picture, and someone in this picture has a problem.

You tell me what you think the problem might be.

*Show children Illustration 19.*

(Child 1), what do you think the problem might be? (*If needed:* Who do you think has the problem?)

Why do you think _____? (*Repeat the child's stated problem. If needed:* What do you think might have happened that led up to this situation?)

Who sees a DIFFERENT problem?

*Repeat the previous questions with another child.*

Do (Child 1) and (Child 2) see the SAME problem or a DIFFERENT problem?

*If different:* See, two people can see the SAME things and think DIFFERENT things are happening.

*If the same:* Who sees a DIFFERENT problem?

*After children run out of responses:*

If these were real people, how could you find out what the problem really is? (*Elicit asking as a way to find out.*)

What did we learn from this?

What do we have to find out about what we see before we really know what a problem is?

ILLUSTRATION 19  Lesson 34

# Do You Remember a Time When . . .

## PURPOSE

To provide a review of pre-problem-solving skills for application
in actual situations

## MATERIALS

None

## TEACHER SCRIPT

*If desired, remind children of the lessons to which the following questions
relate. Lesson numbers are given in parentheses after each question.*

Can you think of a time when:

1. You and another person felt the SAME way about
   the SAME thing? (Lessons 4 and 5)

2. You and another person felt DIFFERENT ways about
   the SAME thing? (Lessons 4 and 5)

3. Someone gave you part of a message, not the whole message,
   so you got the wrong message? (Lessons 7 and 8)

4. You didn't hear something important because you were NOT
   listening? (Lessons 9 and 12)

5. It was a good idea to wait and NOT be impatient? (Lesson 10)

6. You found out what someone's problem was by listening
   to him or her talk? (Lesson 20)

7. You found out what someone's problem was by watching
   what he or she did? (Lesson 20)

8. You found out what someone's problem was by asking
   him or her? (Lesson 21)

9. Someone thought you liked something (for example, a gift),
   but you did NOT like it? (Lesson 31)

10. You thought someone liked something, but he or she
    did NOT? (Lesson 31)

11. Someone got ANGRY at you for the wrong reason? (Lesson 31)

12. You got ANGRY at somebody else for the wrong reason? (Lesson 31)

13. Someone thought you did something, but you did NOT? (Lesson 33)

14. You thought someone did something, but that person did NOT? (Lesson 33)

## OPTIONS

1. Read the questions aloud and let children discuss them in the group. Continue, a few each day, until all have been covered.

2. Write three questions at a time on the chalkboard. Let children pick two questions to write or think about. Have them read or tell the group their responses. Repeat this process until all the questions have been covered.

## SAMPLE RESPONSE

*This answer was written by a sixth grader in response to Question 12, "Can you think of a time when you got ANGRY at somebody else for the wrong reason?" (Lesson 31).*

Once there were two best friends, Jennifer and Nurahdin.

So one day someone wrote a letter and gave it to me and said:

> Dear Nurahdin,
>
> I am not your friend anymore.
>
> Yours truly,
> Jennifer

But Jennifer didn't write it. Anyway, I wrote back and said:

> Dear Jennifer,
>
> Well, I don't want to be your friend either.
>
> Nurahdin

Then Jennifer came to me and said, "Why don't you want to be my friend?" I showed her the letter, and she said, "I didn't write this." I said, "You didn't? Well, who did?" I asked everyone in my classroom [if Jennifer wrote it]. Everyone said, "No." I said, "I'm sorry, Jennifer. I feel so embarrassed."

ICPS: I could have asked Jennifer did she write this note instead of accusing her.

# Review of Pre-Problem-Solving Concepts

## PURPOSE

To review ICPS concepts taught thus far

## MATERIALS

Chalkboard or easel

Feeling Word List (see Lesson 15)

Any two hand puppets (optional)

## TEACHER SCRIPT

*Write the Feeling Word List on the chalkboard (or refer to a previously prepared poster).*

When somebody starts talking when someone else is talking,
what are they doing to the person who is trying to talk?
(*If needed:* Are they listening or interrupting?)

OK, I'm going to show you a play, and you try to figure out how
*both* people in the play are feeling and what they're thinking.

*Have the two puppets act out the following exchange. If any of the children in the group are named Robert or Tommy, be sure to change the puppets' names. If puppets are not available, use paper bags or socks, let children make their own puppets, or have two children take the parts.*

| | |
|---|---|
| Teacher: | This is Robert. This is Tommy. *(Make both puppets bow.)* |
| Robert: | *(Turns toward Tommy.)* Tommy, you said you'd play videogames with me yesterday, and you didn't come. You let me down, and I feel DISAPPOINTED. I also feel ANGRY at you. |
| Tommy: | I couldn't come. I . . . |
| Robert: | *(Interrupts.)* Well, I waited and waited, and now I don't want to speak to you anymore. *(Move puppet as if walking away.)* |
| Tommy: | *(Moves toward Robert.)* If you'd listen to me, I can tell you . . . |
| Robert: | *(Puts head down, very sadly.)* |

It's understandable that Robert feels DISAPPOINTED and even ANGRY.

What else might Robert have said or asked Tommy before getting so mad he wouldn't even talk to him? Raise your hand if you can think of something. *(Call on a child.)*

How might Tommy feel when Robert interrupts him and won't even let him talk? *(Let the group answer.)*

What might Tommy have said if he had not been interrupted and could have talked? Raise your hand if you can tell us. *(Call on a child.)*

How might Robert feel then? *(Let the group answer.)*

OK, now we're going to change this game a little.

I wonder how one person might talk to another when one of them won't share something.

Who wants to come up and play the puppets?

*Let one child play the role of both puppets, or have two children act out the parts. Encourage the children to have the puppets tell each other their feelings and why they feel that way. Have them refer to the Feeling Word List as needed.*

*If more than two puppets are available, let children choose among them. After this situation has been role-played, invite children to act out the next two scenarios.*

I wonder how people might tell each other how they feel and why, when one of them bullies the other.

Who wants to come up and role-play this situation?

Now we need someone to make one puppet interrupt the other one. But whoever does this has to make up something to interrupt.

Who wants to try it?

*After children have acted out the interrupting scenario, have them replay the situation, this time letting each puppet talk.*

# Problem-Solving Skills

# ALTERNATIVE SOLUTIONS

The lessons in this section help children learn that there is more than one way to solve a problem. In particular, they stimulate children to think of as many different solutions as possible to everyday interpersonal problems and encourage a *process* of thinking: "There's more than one way"; "I don't have to give up too soon."

## PROCEDURE

As used in the lessons, the general procedure for eliciting alternative solutions is as follows:

1. State the problem or have the child state the problem.

2. Say that the idea is to think of lots of DIFFERENT ways to solve this problem.

3. Write all of the children's ideas on chalkboard or easel.

4. Ask for the first solution. If the solution is relevant, repeat it and identify it as *one* way to solve the problem. Remind children that the object is to think of lots of DIFFERENT ways to solve the problem.

5. Ask for another solution, and so forth.

6. When ideas run out, probe for further solutions by asking, "What can _____ say to *(repeat problem)*" and "What can _____ do to *(repeat problem)*?"

## ENUMERATIONS

Children often give variations of the same solution. For example:

- *Giving something:* Give him candy, give him ice cream, give him presents.

- *Returning a favor:* Carry her books, walk her to school, help her with her homework.

- *Hurting someone:* Hit him, fight, beat him up.

An effective way of dealing with enumerations is to say, for example, "Giving candy and giving presents are both kind of the SAME because they are both giving something. Can you think of something DIFFERENT from giving something?" After a while, you can ask children to identify for themselves how enumerations show the same kinds of ideas.

Avoid saying, "That's good" or "That's a good idea" in response to a given solution. If you focus on the *content* of what children say, they will think you like a particular idea and you will likely get more enumerations. If you do say *good,* focus on the *process* by saying, "Good, that's a DIFFERENT idea."

A child may disagree as to whether a given response is or is not an enumeration of a previously given solution. Everyone does not have to agree, but be sure to ask why the child feels as he or she does. The idea is to promote thinking about the situation. Lively, stimulating discussions can result.

## UNCLEAR OR APPARENTLY IRRELEVANT RESPONSES

If a child gives an unclear or apparently irrelevant response, it is important to ask, "Why do you think that will solve this problem?" or to say, "Tell us a little more about that." Often a response that is unclear or seems irrelevant is actually quite logical.

Take, for instance, the problem of a boy's parents ignoring him when he asks them to help him with his homework. The solution "Pass the salt" may seem irrelevant. However, if you ask, "How would that help get the boy's parents to help him with his homework?" the child might say, "Tell them breakfast is ready. And while they're eating breakfast, they'll say, 'Pass the salt.' And he'll say he'll pass the salt if they'll help him with his homework. That's how he can get their attention."

"He will cry" is another response requiring clarification. If the response is simply a *reaction* to the problem's existence, it is irrelevant because it is not a solution to the problem. If, on the other hand, the response is intended to gain sympathy, it is a *cognitive cry*—and therefore a solution. If a child gives this response, always ask him or her to tell you more.

# It Takes Time to Think

## PURPOSE

To introduce alternative solution and consequential thinking

To help children begin to recognize that problems cannot always be solved quickly and that the first idea one thinks of may not always be the best one

## MATERIALS

Pencils and paper

## TEACHER SCRIPT

Today we're going to see what happens when we do and do NOT take time to think about something.

Here's a problem between two people: Person A made Person B ANGRY because Person A spilled food on Person B's clothes.

*Have children take out pencils and paper.*

Everybody write a solution.

A *solution* is a way to solve a problem—in this case so Person B won't be ANGRY anymore.

Write it down, very quickly.

*Allow only 5 seconds for children to respond.*

OK, now let's do this again, only this time, stop and think of a really good idea.

When you think of a good idea, write it down.

*Allow more time for children to respond.*

If you think your first idea is better than your second one, raise your hand.

If you think your second idea is better than your first one, raise your hand.

*(Regardless of whether more thought their first or second idea was better)* Sometimes it takes time to think, and the first thing that pops into your head is not always the best thing to do.

*Ask a child to read both of his or her solutions.*

(To the child) Which solution do you think is better?

Why?

Does anyone have a DIFFERENT opinion about which
one is better? Why?

*Let a few more children read their solutions. Ask them the same questions you
did the first child.*

Can you think of a time when you did something to solve
a problem and later thought of a better way?

Tell us about it.

---

**HINT**

Be sure not to place any value judgments on what the children say.
Let the children hear the pros and cons (as stated by them) for each
solution offered.

---

214

# There's More Than One Way, Part I

## PURPOSE

To illustrate that there is more than one way to solve a problem and that if one way is not successful, it is possible to try a DIFFERENT way

## MATERIALS

Chalkboard or easel

## TEACHER SCRIPT

In our ICPS lessons so far, we have talked a lot about the idea that there is more than one.

We have seen that there is more than one way to find out how people feel.

Do you remember them? (*If needed:* By watching/seeing, listening/hearing, and asking.)

We have seen that there is more than one reason people may do things, such as not say hello.

There is also more than one way to solve a problem between people.

I'm going to tell you a problem that came up between children. Then you tell us how the child in the story could solve the problem—you know, what the child could do or say.

The idea is to think of lots of ways, lots of DIFFERENT ways the child could solve the problem.

*Draw the following stick figures on the chalkboard.*

This boy (*point to the figure alone*) wants to join the group in a game of tag, but the others are not paying any attention to him.

Now, what is the problem here? *(Let a child repeat the problem.)*

What can this boy do or say to get into the game?

Remember, we want to think of lots of DIFFERENT ways.

I'll write your ideas on the chalkboard.

*Write each response as given to form a numbered list.*

RESPONSE: He could ask. *(Write this on the board, as the example shows.)*

1. He could ask.

*If response is relevant:* That's *one* way. Now the idea of this game is to think of lots of DIFFERENT ways to solve the problem.

*If response is not relevant:* How would that help solve the problem?

OK, he could ask. That's *one* way.

*Emphasize the word* one *when saying, "That's* one *way," in this and subsequent lessons to suggest the possibility of other alternatives.*

Now the idea of this game is to think of lots of DIFFERENT ways this boy can get the other kids to let him play tag with them.

Who's got way number two? Let's put lots of ideas on the board.

RESPONSE: He could say, "I'll invite you to my house." *(Add to the list.)*

1. He could ask.
2. He could say he'll invite them to his house.

OK, he could ask, or he could say he'll invite the kids to his house. Now we have two ways.

I bet you can think of lots of DIFFERENT ways.

Who can think of way three?

RESPONSE: He could say he'll let them come to his birthday party. *(Enumeration—write under the like response, not as a separate solution.)*

216

> 1. He could ask.
> 2. He could say he'll invite them to his house.
>    He could say he'll invite them to his birthday party.

Oh, inviting the kids to his house and inviting them to his birthday party are *enumerations*.

In other words, they are kind of the SAME because _____.
(*If needed:* They are both examples of inviting the kids to do something.)

Who can think of something DIFFERENT from giving an invitation?

RESPONSE: He could walk away crying. *(Unclear response—clarify.)*

Tell me more about that.

RESPONSE: So they'll feel sorry for him. *(Add to the list.)*

> 1. He could ask.
> 2. He could say he'll invite them to his house.
>    He could say he'll invite them to his birthday party.
> 3. He could walk away crying so they'll feel sorry for him.

*If the child says the boy would walk away crying because the other kids won't let him play, the response may be irrelevant because it could be just his reaction to the situation—and thus not a solution to the problem. Say, "He might walk away crying. Tell me more about that." In this case, the clarification "So they'll feel sorry for him" suggests that the response is a way to get the kids to give in—and therefore a relevant solution.*

OK, he could walk away crying so the kids will feel sorry for him and let him play. That's way three.

Who has a DIFFERENT way?

RESPONSE: He could say he'll make them happy.
            *(Unclear response—clarify.)*

Tell me more about that.

RESPONSE: He could say he'll be "It." *(Add to the list.)*

1. He could ask.
2. He could say he'll invite them to his house.
   He could say he'll invite them to his birthday party.
3. He could walk away crying so they'll feel sorry for him.
4. He could make them happy by saying he'll be "It."

*If a general solution like "make them happy" is given, be sure to clarify. Ask, "How could he do that?" or "How could he find out if the kids would be happy?"*

OK, we have four ways this boy can try to get these kids
to let him play tag with them.

*Summarize all the solutions presented thus far and encourage further solutions, writing each one on the board. When children run out of solutions, draw the following stick figures on the board, then repeat the procedure conducted for the first situation.*

This girl's name is Susan.

Susan's mother went to work, then Susan went to the store
to buy her mother a book she had asked for.

But Susan bought the wrong book, and now her mother
is ANGRY. What can Susan do or say so her mother won't
be ANGRY?

---

**HINT**

It is better to let a slower class offer all their ideas, then classify
enumerations at the end. Teachers of such classes have found
reading each idea on the board, then asking, "Whose idea was this?"
a good motivating technique.

---

# There's More Than One Way, Part II

## PURPOSE

To strengthen the idea that there is more than one way to solve a problem and that if one way is not successful, it is possible to try a DIFFERENT way

## MATERIALS

Chalkboard or easel

## TEACHER SCRIPT

*Follow the procedure outlined in Lesson 38 for the additional problem situations presented here. For the first one, draw stick figures on the chalkboard as before.*

Let's say the problem here is that this girl *(point to the sister)* wants to watch her favorite television program, but her brother *(point)* is watching another program.

What can the sister do or say so she can have a chance to watch her program?

*After children have generated a number of alternative solutions:*

> Who can think of a problem between people?

> This could be a real problem that happened to you or to someone you know, or you could just make it up.

*When a problem seems suitable for eliciting alternative solutions, let the child who proposed it draw it on the board in the form of stick figures. Perhaps with guidance that child could lead the group in generating solutions. Repeat with as many children as time and interest permit.*

---

**HINT**

If a generally responsive child repeats another child's idea, casually say, "I bet you can think of a DIFFERENT idea." If a generally non-responsive child repeats another child's idea, say, "Good, you told us, too." Do not push for a different solution at this time. It is important to praise the child for having said something. Judge later when it would be helpful to ask for a different solution.

---

# Writing and Drawing Alternative Solutions

## PURPOSE

To encourage children to think about solutions to interpersonal problems as they come up in real life

## MATERIALS

Paper and pencils

## TEACHER SCRIPT

Who can remember a time you had a problem with someone at home, on the playground, or at lunch? *(Let several children respond.)*

How did you try to solve the problem?

Did your *first* idea work?

What finally happened?

*Discuss a few examples, then encourage children to write or draw their own real-life problem situation. After they have finished, have them share with the class.*

*Encourage them to try thinking of alternative solutions at home with siblings and friends, and to report to the group about what they did and what happened.*

## SAMPLE SOLUTION STORY

*The following story was written by a fifth grader.*

My cousin Sandra and Ayesha were arguing over a coin because they found it at the same time. Then they were fighting. Ayesha knocked Sandra down the steps. Then Ayesha's mother and Sandra's mother got in an argument. But Sandra's mother yelled at Ayesha's mother first. And they got in a fight, and Sandra's mother got beat up and knocked out the door, and Ayesha was laughing, and Sandra was crying. And Ayesha slapped Sandra in the face, and they were fighting again. Janet came in and stopped it. Sandra's mother came in and knocked Janet down. And punched her.

## Solutions

1. Ayesha could have let Sandra have the coin even though it was 10 cents.

2. Ayesha or Sandra could have stopped fighting before Sandra fell down the steps.

3. The fight would have never started if this didn't happen.

4. If the arguments hadn't started there wouldn't be fighting.

5. The only time Sandra's mother lost her ICPS is when she yelled at Ayesha's mother and the fighting.

This girl had a problem

Her problem is that the boy and girl wont play with her what will she do?

No

plesae give me The pocte Book

# What Can I Do? A Story

## PURPOSE

To apply skills in perspective taking to a problem-solving situation

## MATERIALS

Chalkboard or easel

Mini-Play 11

## TEACHER SCRIPT

> **NOTE**
> Make a copy of Mini-Play 11 for each actor, then circle each actor's part.

Remember our story about Tara, Rachel, and Paulette?

Today we're going to take that story a little further.

Remember, Rachel opened Paulette's birthday present, and Paulette was crying because she saw someone had opened it.

Tara was the one who bought it and wrapped it, right?

*If desired, redraw the figures illustrated in Lesson 31.*

Who remembers what Tara thought when she saw Paulette crying over the opened present? (*If needed:* Tara thought Paulette didn't like the present.)

OK, let's continue this story. Remember, Tara did NOT find out why Paulette was crying.

*Choose three children to act out the parts in Mini-Play 11, then write the following questions on the chalkboard:*

1. What's the problem?
2. When does the problem come up?
3. How does each person feel?

*(To the group)* As the story is being acted out, listen for the problem and when it comes up in the story.

Think about how each person in the story feels.

*After children have acted out the mini-play, ask the three questions you wrote on the board, then let the actors make up the end of the story so everyone feels happy. If needed, review the idea that Tara yelled at Paulette before Tara knew that Rachel opened the present. Point out that Paulette felt Tara was mad at her for the wrong reason.*

## THE BIRTHDAY PRESENT REVISITED

Tara:   Paulette, I thought for a long time about what to get you for your birthday. You always said you wanted a paint set, and that's what I got you. I spent a lot of money on it, too. Now you don't like it, and I'm never going to get you anything again!

Paulette:   But . . .

Tara:   You can't get out of it now. I saw you crying. You're just a big crybaby anyway.

Paulette:   You're stupid! I don't want to talk to you now either!

Rachel:   *(Entering)* Uh-oh. I hear them. I'd better do something about this. It's all my fault.

*Finish this mini-play so everyone feels happy.*

# There's More Than One Way, Part III

## PURPOSE

To help children generate alternative solutions and identify enumerations

## MATERIALS

Chalkboard or easel

Illustration 20

## TEACHER SCRIPT

Today's ICPS lesson is about solving a problem.

*Show children Illustration 20.*

This boy (Tom) punched this other boy (Dan) and knocked him down.
Ben *(point)* thinks to himself, "I can help them solve this problem."

What does Ben have to find out before he can help them?

*Elicit the idea that Ben must know why Tom punched Dan.*

OK, tell me a reason that Tom might have punched Dan.

*Have children generate several reasons. Choose one, or let the class choose one.*

OK. Let's say the problem is _____.
(*For example:* Dan won't let Tom fly his model airplanes.)

To figure out how Ben can help them solve this problem,
we're going to have two teams.

Here's how we'll play. First, someone from Team A will give
us a solution, and I will write it on the chalkboard.

Then someone from Team B will give us a solution, and I will
write that on the board.

Listen carefully and look at the board.

If the solution from Team B is an *enumeration* of what the person
from Team A said, or kind of the SAME, try to catch it.

We'll give the person who caught the enumeration a chance to
give a DIFFERENT solution.

If that person can't come up with a new solution, we'll go back to Team B.

As we go along, try not to give an enumeration of any solution already on the board.

Anyone in the class can catch an enumeration: If you catch an enumeration, try to tell us why you think it is one.

*Divide the group into two teams. Alternate asking Team A and Team B for solutions until both teams run out of ideas. Write all responses on the board— different relevant solutions, enumerations, unclear or apparently irrelevant responses. Then classify responses as the following example shows.*

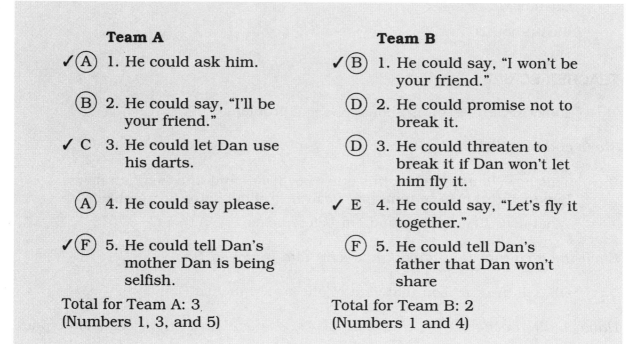

**Team A**

✓ (A) 1. He could ask him.

(B) 2. He could say, "I'll be your friend."

✓ C 3. He could let Dan use his darts.

(A) 4. He could say please.

✓ (F) 5. He could tell Dan's mother Dan is being selfish.

Total for Team A: 3
(Numbers 1, 3, and 5)

**Team B**

✓ (B) 1. He could say, "I won't be your friend."

(D) 2. He could promise not to break it.

(D) 3. He could threaten to break it if Dan won't let him fly it.

✓ E 4. He could say, "Let's fly it together."

(F) 5. He could tell Dan's father that Dan won't share

Total for Team B: 2
(Numbers 1 and 4)

*In the example, the same circled letters are enumerations; the ones with check marks are original solutions.*

*Note that Team A receives credit for its fifth response and Team B does not. Whichever team suggests the solution first gets the point.*

*Note also that Team A's second response and Team B's first one are reverse enumerations. Thus, Team B receives the credit, and Team A does not. Explain these by saying, for example, " 'I'll be your friend' and 'I won't be your friend,' are kind of the SAME because they're both a way to bargain friendship. One is just the opposite of the other. Can you think of something DIFFERENT from bargaining friendship?''*

*Promising not to break the plane and threatening to break it (both Team B responses) are also reverse enumerations. Ask, "Can you think of something DIFFERENT from the plane's being or not being broken?"*

*If time and interest permit, name a new problem, or have a child name one. Let the child who volunteered the problem draw it on the board. Generate solutions and analyze enumerations as before.*

---

**HINT**

If children disagree about whether or not something is an enumeration, encourage discussion. If any enumerations are not caught by the class, point them out. You can decide, depending on the nature of your class, if you want to note which team "won" because they had the most different, relevant solutions.

---

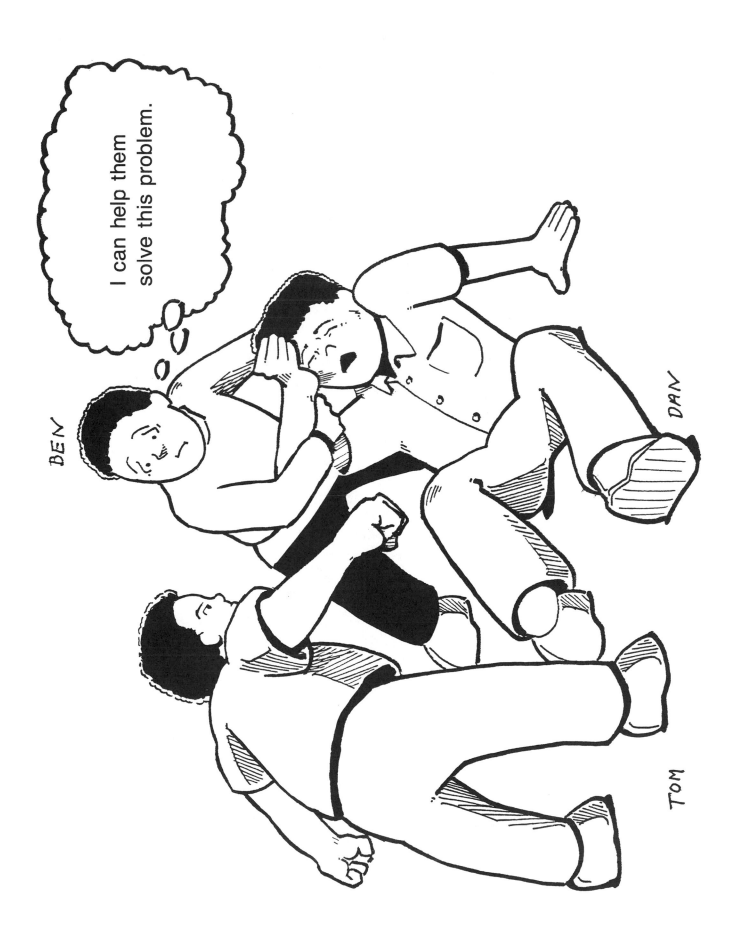

ILLUSTRATION 20  Lesson 42

# Feeling Cartoons, Part II

## PURPOSE

To give children practice in thinking about what makes DIFFERENT people feel the SAME way (the opposite of Lesson 18)

## MATERIALS

Activity Sheets 14 and 15

## TEACHER SCRIPT

*Give each child a copy of Activity Sheets 14 and 15.*

This ICPS game is like the one we played before with cartoon balloons.

These are DIFFERENT people feeling the SAME way.

How do you think they look and feel? *(Let children answer.)*

Right, ANGRY.

OK. Who is looking ANGRY in the first picture?

Yes, the girl about your age.

And in the second?

Yes, the father.

The third?

Yes, the mother.

And the fourth?

OK, the boy about your age.

Try to think of DIFFERENT things that these people might be thinking about that makes them feel ANGRY.

Write these thoughts in the cartoon balloons above each person.

**OPTIONS**

1. When finished, let a child read his or her thoughts for one character. Help the group classify enumerations. If you write the child's thoughts on the chalkboard, the rest of the group can see which of their own ideas were the same, were enumerations, or were different.

2. Pair children and let them read their responses to each other. They can circle any of the same ideas in their cartoon balloons.

3. Display filled-in illustrations on a bulletin board.

# Role-Playing, Part II

## PURPOSE

To help children experience independent problem-solving thinking, this time as relates to an actual problem

## MATERIALS

None

## TEACHER SCRIPT

Today we're going to role-play a real problem that you had with someone.

It can be a classmate, someone at home—anyone.

OK. Who has a problem? *(Call on one child.)*

Now _____, tell us the people you need to role-play your problem.

If the problem is with a classmate or classmates and if they're here, pick them.

If they're not here, or if the problem is with someone else, pick someone to play their parts.

*After all the actors are chosen:*

OK, go plan your role-play for a few minutes.

First, plan how you'll show us what the problem is.

Then plan how to act out your solution.

*Encourage children to act out the problem. If the main actor has trouble solving the problem, ask whether someone from the group can join in and help. After the role-play:*

Can you think of a time when you tried to make someone feel better and you had to try more than one way?

What about when someone tried to solve a problem for you that you could have solved yourself?

**HINT**

From now on, when actual problems come up, you may wish to let the children involved role-play the situation. Encourage the role-players and the class to solve the problem.

# ICPS Tic-Tac-Toe

## PURPOSE

To give children practice in generating solutions and identifying enumerations

To help children classify the nature of problems and ways to solve them

## MATERIALS

Chalkboard or easel

## TEACHER SCRIPT

Today we're going to play the game tic-tac-toe in a special way. But first, as a warm-up, we'll play it the regular way.

Who knows how to play this game?

*Draw a tic-tac-toe box on the chalkboard. If anyone does not know how to play, pick two children and have them demonstrate how the game is played in the usual way.*

OK. Now we're going to play this game in a new way.

I'm going to tell you a problem.

The *X* person thinks of lots of solutions, one for each square.

The *O* person thinks of lots of solutions, too.

Each person takes a turn picking a square and giving a solution.

If the person gives a DIFFERENT solution, he or she gets to put an *X* or *O* in the square.

If the person gives an enumeration of a solution already given, an answer that is kind of the SAME, he or she doesn't get the square, and the other player gets a chance.

The other player can then pick the SAME or a DIFFERENT square.

As soon as we put a solution in the square, the rest of you watch and try to catch enumerations.

*Choose two children to come up and play the game. If necessary, remind the group that the object of the game is to be the first one to get three Xs or Os in a line.*

Here's the problem: LeMar was riding Curtis's bicycle and broke the wheel.

He's afraid Curtis will be ANGRY.

What can LeMar do or say so Curtis won't be ANGRY?

*Draw another tic-tac-toe box on the board and write down the players' solutions in the boxes of their choosing. If the solution is an original one, let the player mark an X or O, as the example shows.*

| Put wire on it<br>X | | Fix it<br>*(Enumeration)* |
|---|---|---|
| Say sorry<br>X | Buy a new one<br>O | |
| Give him candy<br>O | | |

*If a child's response is seemingly irrelevant, ask, "How will that help keep Curtis from being ANGRY?" If the response is still irrelevant, erase the idea and ask for a new solution.*

*If an enumeration is offered, write it down and wait for a child to catch it. If a child catches it, ask him or her to explain why it is an enumeration, then erase the enumerated response. (In the sample provided, "Fix it" is an enumeration of "Put wire on it" and should be erased.)*

*The child who catches the enumeration replaces the child who gave it. If the new player can give a different solution, he or she can pick the same or a different square. If no one catches the enumeration, point it out yourself. If you point out the enumeration, let the original players continue.*

*If time permits, let children make up a problem and repeat the game.*

---

**HINT**

Children enjoy gathering in small groups to play this game during indoor recess.

---

# What's Wrong With What They Say?

## PURPOSE

To help children think more about taking the perspective of another person

## MATERIALS

None

## TEACHER SCRIPT

I'm going to say some things, and if you can tell us what's wrong with the statement, raise your hand.

George Washington said, "I'm going to fly over the Delaware River in a jet plane."

What's wrong with that?

*If someone says George Washington doesn't need a jet plane to fly over the river, ask, "What else is wrong with that statement?"*

Abraham Lincoln told (name current President), "I like to watch you on television."

What's wrong with that?

What else is wrong with that?

Janie, 4 years old, gave her mother a brand new doll for her birthday.

What's wrong with that?

Susan was the first one to get up one morning.

She found her dog had died during the night.

She woke up her mother and said, "Why didn't you tell me the dog died last night?"

What's wrong with that?

How do you think Susan's mother felt at that moment, other than SAD because the dog died?

How might Susan have felt when she found out her mother really didn't know the dog had died?

George lives in _____. (*Name a city or town that is far away.*)

There is a blizzard there—you know, a big snowstorm.

George calls up his friend, Rudy, on the telephone.

Rudy lives in _____. (*Name your own city or town.*)

George tells Rudy he can't come visit him because the airplanes aren't flying in the blizzard.

Rudy looks out the window in _____ and sees it's a beautiful, sunny day.

He goes back to the telephone and says, "George, it's a beautiful day. There's no snow, and you're just lying. You don't want to come and visit me!"

What's wrong with that?

Can anyone make up something else so we could ask, "What's wrong with that?"

*Continue as time and interest permit.*

# Alternative Solutions

**MINI-DIALOGUE: ONE CHILD**

**Situation:** Josh won't share his plastic turtles with Walter.

Teacher: What's the problem? What's wrong?[1]

Walter: He won't share his turtles.

Teacher: What did you do?

Walter: I grabbed 'em.

Teacher: How did Josh feel when you did that?[2]

Walter: Mad!

Teacher: How did *you* feel about this?[2]

Walter: Frustrated and mad.

Teacher: Grabbing is *one* thing you can do.
Can you think of something DIFFERENT
to do so he won't be mad?[3]

Walter: I could let him use my football.

Teacher: How can you find out if he'd like that?[4]

Walter: I could ask him.

Teacher: Go ahead and try that.

## NOTES

[1] Gets the child's perspective on the problem.

[2] Guides thought about own and others' feelings. These questions say to a child: Someone cares how I feel. Someone cares what I think.

[3] Helps the child think of alternative solutions.

[4] Guides the child to think about how to find out others' preferences.

## MINI-DIALOGUE: TWO CHILDREN

**Situation:** Keshia will not share her ruler with Sondra.

Teacher:   What's happening? What's the problem?
That will help me understand the
problem better.[1]

Sondra:   She's selfish. She won't let me use her ruler,
and I share my things with her.

Keshia:   I need it. She won't give it back.
She never gives things back.

Teacher:   Sondra, how do you feel about this?[2]

Sondra:   Frustrated!

Teacher:   Keshia, how do *you* feel about this?[2]

Keshia:   Mad!

Teacher:   Can you two think of a way to solve this problem
so Sondra won't feel frustrated and Keshia won't
feel mad?[3]

Sondra:   I'll just use it for a minute. You can stand
right here, and I'll give it right back.

Keshia:   OK.

Teacher:   Good, you solved the problem yourselves.
How do you feel about that?[4]

## NOTES

[1] Gets children's points of view.

[2] Guides children to think about feelings.

[3] Guides children to think of alternative solutions.

[4] Acknowledges children's solution and encourages them to evaluate
how they feel now that the problem is solved.

*Children learn best by carrying out their own solutions. If Sondra and Keshia
had not been able to find a solution, the teacher could have brought in another
child to help. Sometimes children learn more if a peer suggests a solution than
if a teacher does so.*

# What's the Problem?

*The following examples will help children understand what a problem really is by illustrating what is and what is not important to know.*

**Example 1:** An elevator has a sign reading "1,500 Pounds Maximum Weight." That means the sum of all the weight on the elevator cannot be more than 1,500 pounds.

1. Two men and one woman get on.
2. Mr. Aaron has brown hair.
3. Mr. Aaron weighs 250 pounds.
4. Mr. Smith has a speech problem.
5. Mr. Smith weighs 135 pounds.
6. Ms. Green weighs 102 pounds.
7. Someone puts an elephant on that weighs 1,210 pounds.
8. The elephant's name is Flapper.
9. Flapper came from the circus.

Which of these statements are needed to know what the problem is?

Which statements are NOT needed?

What is the problem here?

**Example 2:** It is 0 degrees Fahrenheit outside.

1. Ms. Parker, age 25, is wearing a blue dress.
2. Ms. Jones, age 31, is wearing gray slacks.
3. Mr. Peters, age 23, is wearing an orange shirt.
4. Jackson, age 10, is wearing a yellow jacket.

Are these four people too cold?

What important information is missing? NOT here?

What information given is NOT needed to answer this question?

*Let the group make up other examples. In addition, use stories read in class. Identify a problem and state what is and is not needed to identify and/or solve a problem.*

# More Than One

## READING AND STORY COMPREHENSION

Why did (Character 1) do or say _____?
*(Describe something the character did or said.)*

Why might (Character 1) have done or said that?

Any other possible reason?

How did (Character 1) feel when (he/she) did that?

Is there any other way (he/she) might have felt?

What might (Character 2) have thought to (himself/herself)
when (Character 1) did or said that?

What else might (he/she) have thought about that?

## MATH

### Sums

How many combinations of numbers can you think of to equal 30?

*Give examples as needed to get the class started, based on what your group
is learning. For example:*

$$\left(\frac{1}{3} \times 60\right) + 10$$

$$\frac{1}{2} \text{ of } 60$$

$$\frac{180}{6}$$

$$5 \times 6$$

$$(6 \times 6) - 6$$

$$XV + XV$$

*Let children make up other totals and ways to reach them. Invite children to
put their ideas up on the chalkboard. If correct, say, "That's one way. Who has
a DIFFERENT way?"*

**Arrangement Alternatives**

*Draw the following on the chalkboard.*

Row 1: • • • • • • • • • •

Row 2: (pennies arranged in a circle)

Row 3: • • • • • • • • • •

Here are some pennies.

Without counting, are there the SAME number or
a DIFFERENT number of pennies in Row 1 and Row 2?

In Row 1 and Row 3?

How did you decide on your answers?

Can you think of any other ways to arrange 10 pennies?

## SCIENCE

The following could have happened for more than one reason.

The plant died because . . .

- Someone didn't water it.
- The water was too hot.
- There was (not enough/too much) food.
- There was (not enough/too much) light.
- Insects ate the roots.

Think of more than one reason that . . .

- A fish dies.
- A tree limb breaks.
- Someone misses the basket when he or she shoots the basketball.

## SOCIAL STUDIES

There's more than one reason that . . .

- Someone would want to be a (police officer/fire fighter).
- (Marquette/Joliet) might have explored the Mississippi River.
- People might move from one area to another.

# Classification

*Classifying ideas in academic areas can help children understand similarities and differences in the interpersonal arena.*

**OPTION 1**

*Write the following words on the chalkboard and ask children how they are the same. Let children add to each list once the criterion for classification has been identified.*

Springfield

Harrisburg

Albany

NOT Philadelphia

ANSWER: The first three are capital cities.

Asia

Africa

North America

NOT Spain

ANSWER: The first three are continents.

Saw
Second
Clown
Well
NOT snow

ANSWER: All but *snow* are words with more than one possible meaning, spelled and pronounced the SAME way.

Desert
Wind
Minute
Content
NOT orange

ANSWER: All but *orange* are words with more than one meaning, spelled alike but pronounced a DIFFERENT way.

Philadelphia
New York
Boston
NOT San Francisco

ANSWER: The first three are cities in the eastern United States.

## OPTION 2

*Divide the group into two teams. Read the first item on the list aloud and wait for an attempt to classify. Then read the second, and so forth. Whichever team first figures out a relevant criterion for classification wins the point.*

### State Capitals

Springfield

Harrisburg

Albany

### Things to Read

Book

Magazine

Newspaper

Comics

### Sports Played Without a Ball

Discus

Pole vaulting

High jumping

Auto racing

Horse racing

*If needed:* NOT basketball, NOT football

### Other Ideas

Individual versus team sports

Living versus deceased Presidents of the United States

All Presidents who served after 1950

Things made of rubber (or metal)

Things that are red (or any other color)

## OPTION 3

*Next create categories that have at least two criteria for classification.*

### Example 1

How are the following cities the same?
Boston (Massachusetts) and Providence (Rhode Island)

RESPONSE: Both are capitals.

How else?

RESPONSE: Both are in New England.

*Name or have the class name more capital cities in New England.*

### Example 2

How are the countries Liechtenstein and Switzerland the same?

RESPONSE: Both are in Western Europe.

How else?

RESPONSES: Both have lots of mountains, are famous for skiing, have lots of snow.

*Name or have the class name more countries in Western Europe where people ski, and so on.*

# CONSEQUENCES

The lessons in this section help children understand the possible consequences of a particular solution. A *consequence* is a reaction by Person B in direct relationship to an act performed by Person A. For example, if Sally hits Megan, Megan might, in consequence, choose to hit her back, tell the teacher, or not play with her anymore. The goal of consequential thinking is to help children think about what might happen next if a particular solution was carried out.

To this point, the exchanges between children and teachers have been "mini-dialogues," including some but not all of the steps in full ICPS dialoguing. After Lessons 47 and 48, in which true consequential thinking is first taught, you may begin to conduct full ICPS dialoguing in the classroom. Basically, this involves asking children, "What might happen next" in addition to using the steps already described. Examples of full ICPS dialogues appear after Lesson 48.

## PROCEDURE

As shown in the lessons, you can elicit consequences by undertaking the following steps:

1. State the problem or have the child state the problem.

2. Elicit alternative solutions in the usual way.

3. When a solution conducive to asking for consequences comes up, use that one. (Usually, "hit," "grab," or "tell someone" are good ones to start with.)

4. Write this solution on the left side of chalkboard or easel.

5. Say, "OK, let's make up a DIFFERENT kind of story. Pretend the person *(repeat the solution)*. What might happen next in the story?" Be sure to elicit direct consequences only, not *chain reactions*. For instance, if Sally hits Megan, a chain of events may continue: Megan might hit Sally back (a direct consequence), then Sally might throw a book at her. Sally's throwing the book is a chain reaction to hitting back, not the direct consequence of Sally's first hitting Megan. If chaining occurs, point it out. For instance, you could say, "That might happen if Megan hits Sally back. What might happen next when Sally first hits Megan?"

6. Say, "Let's think of lots of things that might happen next if *(repeat solution)*. I'm going to write all the things that might happen next on the board. Let's put down lots of ideas." Write these consequences in a column on the right side of the board and draw arrows from the solution to them, as the example shows.

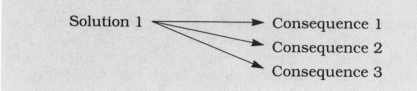

Solution 1 ⟶ Consequence 1
Consequence 2
Consequence 3

7. If necessary, probe for further consequences by asking, "What might _____ say? What might _____ do?"

## ENUMERATIONS

As they do when asked for alternative solutions, children often give consequences that are variations on a theme. Classify these responses in the same way you would solutions, pointing out that the responses are "all kind of the SAME." Ask for "something that might happen that is DIFFERENT" from the enumerated response.

## UNCLEAR OR APPARENTLY IRRELEVANT RESPONSES

Handle unclear or seemingly irrelevant responses in the same way as for alternative solutions. Find out what the child has in mind. A response such as "get mad" to Elizabeth's problem of not getting a turn jumping rope (presented in Lesson 47) could be a simple *reaction* to not having a turn, a *solution* (maybe then the other children will give in and let her have a turn), or a *consequence* to a proposed solution (the other children will be mad if she just butts in). To distinguish whether something is a solution or a consequence, ask who is performing the action. If the child means that Elizabeth gets mad (a reaction or solution), you can elicit a consequence by asking, "What might the other kids jumping rope do or say if Elizabeth does that?"

If a response seems irrelevant, be sure to ask for clarification. Suppose, for example, a child responds to the solution that Elizabeth just jump in to get her turn by saying, "They'll tie their shoes." You might clarify by asking, "How would Elizabeth's jumping into the game cause them to tie their shoes?" That response might turn out to be a relevant consequence (for example, "That's how they'll stop their game so she can't jump"). If, after probing, the response does turn out to be irrelevant, you can say, "Yes, they might do that. Remember, we are talking about what might happen next if Elizabeth just jumps in out of turn."

# What Might Happen Next, Part I

## PURPOSE

To introduce the idea of consequences (IF-THEN)

To help children learn to evaluate solutions for themselves, for later recognition that they can choose a more effective one if need be

## MATERIALS

Chalkboard or easel

## TEACHER SCRIPT

We've been talking about what people can do or say to solve a problem and how there's more than one way to solve problems that come up with people.

Now we're going to talk about a new idea—*consequences.*

For consequences, we ask, "What might happen next if someone does or says something?"

Let's start with consequences that do NOT concern people problems.

IF I drop a glass bottle with juice in it, THEN what will probably happen? *(Let children respond.)*

What else might happen?

*Elicit a number of possible consequences—for example, the glass might break, juice might spill, someone's feet might get cut on the glass.*

See, just as there's more than one way to solve a problem, there can be more than one consequence when something happens.

IF I put the cookie jar too near the edge of the shelf, THEN what might happen?

What else?

Who can think of another situation that might have a consequence? *(Let children respond.)*

Now we're going to talk about people problems and consequences to things people do or say.

Are you ready?

I'm going to tell you a problem between some kids.

After you tell us a few things someone could do to solve the problem *(solutions)*, we're going to think about what might happen next— that is, consequences of what a person does.

The idea is to think of lots of DIFFERENT things that might happen next when someone does or says something, OK?

## Problem 1

*Draw the following stick figures on the chalkboard to illustrate the problem.*

ELIZABETH

Doesn't know how to get into the game

Waiting their turn

The problem is that Elizabeth *(point)* wants to jump rope with these other kids, but she doesn't know how to get into the game.

First, we'll think of lots of solutions for Elizabeth.

*Elicit a number of solutions, as in Lesson 38. Write each solution on the board. Pick one solution from this list—for example, "She could just jump in."*

Let's talk about the solution just to jump in.

If Elizabeth just jumps in, what might the consequences be?

That is, what might happen next?

RESPONSE: They might get mad.

OK, the other kids might get mad. I'm going to put that over here, on the right side of the board.

*Write the consequence in relation to the solution as shown, drawing an arrow to it.*

1. She could just jump in. ⟶ 1. The other kids might get mad.

Now let's think of lots of DIFFERENT things that might happen next if Elizabeth just jumps in.

What else might happen?

RESPONSE: They might start a fight. *(Add to the list under the first consequence and draw an arrow as shown.)*

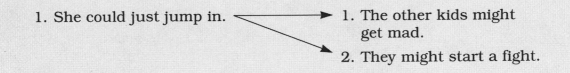

1. She could just jump in. → 1. The other kids might get mad.
   2. They might start a fight.

Yes, that might happen.

The kids might get mad, or they might start a fight.

What else might happen next?

Who has a DIFFERENT consequence?

RESPONSE: They'll start hitting.

*Write enumerations under the like response, not as a separate consequence, as the example shows.*

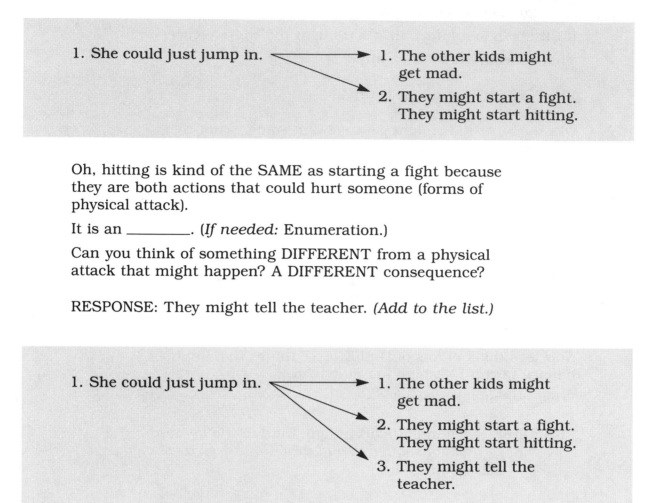

1. She could just jump in. → 1. The other kids might get mad.
   2. They might start a fight. They might start hitting.

Oh, hitting is kind of the SAME as starting a fight because they are both actions that could hurt someone (forms of physical attack).

It is an _____. (*If needed:* Enumeration.)

Can you think of something DIFFERENT from a physical attack that might happen? A DIFFERENT consequence?

RESPONSE: They might tell the teacher. (*Add to the list.*)

1. She could just jump in. → 1. The other kids might get mad.
   2. They might start a fight. They might start hitting.
   3. They might tell the teacher.

*Summarize the potential consequences as each one is suggested, repeating enumerated responses as a single consequence. Clarify any apparently irrelevant consequences by saying, "Tell us more about that" or asking, "Why do you think that might happen?"*

*If a child offers a solution (for example, "She could show them how to jump") write it on the left side of the board with the other solutions. Say, "That's how Elizabeth can get into the game, a solution. The question now is what might happen next if she just jumps in, a consequence."*

*If necessary, probe for further consequences by asking, "What might someone say (or do) if Elizabeth just jumps in?" You may also ask, "How (or how else) might the others feel if Elizabeth just jumps in?" After children run out of ideas:*

Maybe some of you think just jumping in IS a good idea.

Maybe some of you think just jumping in is NOT a good idea.

If you think just jumping in IS a good idea, raise your hand.

*Ask each child who raises a hand why he or she thinks the solution is a good idea. After all have responded:*

If you think just jumping in is NOT a good idea, raise your hand.

*Repeat this line of questioning with all who raise their hands.*

Does anyone want to change his or her mind about whether this IS or is NOT a good idea?

(To any children who raise their hands) Why?

*If desired and if time permits, let the group vote on which of the solutions from the list they initially generated they would like to talk about next.*

## Problem 2

*Draw the following stick figures on the board to illustrate the problem.*

Timmy wants Michael to give him the basketball because it's Timmy's turn to shoot the basket.

The problem is that Michael keeps throwing and won't give up his turn.

*Repeat the line of questioning for Problem 1.*

**Problem 3**

*Draw the following stick figures on the board to illustrate the problem.*

*Let children define the problem for this drawing. (For example, one child does not like the music and wants the other to turn it off.)*

Do these kids feel the SAME way about the SAME thing?

DIFFERENT ways about the SAME thing?

*Continue with the line of questioning for Problem 1. If time and interest permit, you can let a child think of a new problem, draw stick figures on the board, and lead the discussion with your help.*

# Butting In

## PURPOSE

To help children experience independent problem-solving thinking

## MATERIALS

Mini-Play 12

## TEACHER SCRIPT

---

**NOTE**

Make a copy of Mini-Play 12 for each actor, then circle each actor's part. The mini-play includes an example of full ICPS dialoguing, as does the interaction in the classroom example following this lesson. After this lesson, you may integrate full ICPS dialoguing in the classroom.

---

Today we're going to act out a problem situation that comes up sometimes between kids.

We're going to have a mini-play called "Bucky Butt-er-in-er."

I need three boys to act out this play.

I will be the teacher who comes by and sees and hears what's going on.

In this situation, two boys are playing ball, and another boy, Bucky, jumps in front of them and bothers them.

Bucky butts into their games a lot, and that's why they call him Bucky Butt-er-in-er.

The rest of you watch and listen carefully because we'll talk about the scene after it is acted out.

*Tell the children who play Craig and Michael to act out playing ball, then tell the child playing Bucky to act out getting in their way. When the actors have finished performing Mini-Play 12:*

Can anybody think of another solution that Bucky could have tried if what he first tried did NOT work?

What are you going to think about next time a problem like this comes up with someone on the playground? (*If needed:* How people feel, there's more than one solution, there's more than one possible consequence.)

## BUCKY BUTT-ER-IN-ER

*Craig and Michael are playing ball. Bucky butts in.*

|  |  |
|---|---|
| Craig: | Bucky, you're butting in our game! |
| Michael: | You always butt in, and we don't like that. Go away! |
| Bucky: | Ha, ha. You can't even catch a ball. |
| Craig: | You're gonna get it for that! |
| Teacher: | Bucky, what's the problem here? |
| Bucky: | They're threatening me. |
| Teacher: | What led up to that? |
| Bucky: | I don't know. They just are. |
| Teacher: | Craig, how do you see the problem? |
| Craig: | Bucky's butting in our game. |
| Michael: | He always does. |
| Bucky: | Well, they never let me play. |
| Teacher: | Bucky, how do Craig and Michael feel when you do that? |
| Bucky: | Mad. |
| Teacher: | What happened when you tried to butt in? |
| Bucky: | They told me to go away. |
| Teacher: | Butting in is *one* way to get into the game. Can you think of a DIFFERENT way so Michael and Craig won't be mad and won't tell you to go away? |
| Bucky: | I could ask. |
| Teacher: | That's another way. Go ahead and try that. |
| Bucky: | Can I play ball with you? |
| Craig: | No, you still can't play. |
| Teacher: | Uh-oh, it looks like you'll have to think of a DIFFERENT way. |
| Bucky: | *(To Craig)* You can use my bat. |
| Craig: | Well, OK. |
| Teacher: | Good, Bucky, you thought of a way that Craig likes. Find out if that's OK with Michael. |
| Bucky: | *(To Michael)* I'll let you use my bat, too. |
| Michael: | Sure. |
| Teacher: | Bucky, how did you feel before you solved this problem? |
| Bucky: | *(Answers.)* |
| Teacher: | How do you feel now? |
| Bucky: | *(Answers.)* |

# ICPS Dialoguing

## CHILD-CHILD PROBLEMS

**Situation 1:** Pamela and Cynthia are squabbling over a piece of paper.

| | |
|---|---|
| Teacher: | What's the argument about? Tell me about the problem.[1] |
| Pamela: | Cynthia won't give me my paper back. |
| Cynthia: | But I'm not done with it yet. |
| Teacher: | Pamela, trying to grab the paper is *one* way to get it back. What might happen if you do that?[2] |
| Pamela: | It could rip. |
| Teacher: | And how would you feel then?[3] |
| Pamela: | Sad and mad. |
| Teacher: | Can you two think of a DIFFERENT way to solve this problem?[4] |
| Cynthia: | *(To Pamela)* Can I finish drawing on it and then give it back? |
| Pamela: | OK, but just for a little while. |
| Teacher: | Good. You thought of your own way to solve this problem.[5] |

## NOTES

[1] Seeks children's view of the problem.

[2] Guides consequential thinking.

[3] Guides thought about feelings, in this case with regard to a consequence.

[4] Guides alternative solution thinking.

[5] Reinforces not *what* the child thought, but *that* she thought.

**Situation 2:** Three children are drawing on the chalkboard. A fourth child, Dan, starts drawing on Greg's space. Greg elbows Dan, and a fight erupts.

Teacher: OK, kids, you need to calm down so we can talk about this. What's the problem?[1]

Dan: He punched me.

Greg: He got in my way.

Teacher: *(To Dan)* How did you feel when Greg hit you?[2]

Dan: Mad!

Teacher: *(To Greg)* How did you feel when Dan got in your way?[2]

Greg: Mad!

Teacher: OK. You're both mad. And then what happened?[3]

Dan: He could have shared the space.

Greg: He didn't have to butt in.

Dan: He didn't have to hit me.

Teacher: *(To Dan)* What else could you do so Greg might not hit you?[4]

Dan: I could ask him.

Teacher: *(To Greg)* And what else could you have done?[4]

Greg: I could say, "That's my space."

Teacher: *(To both)* OK. What are you two going to do now?

## NOTES

[1] Seeks children's view of the problem.

[2] Guides thought about feelings of both children.

[3] Encourages consequential thinking.

[4] Encourages generation of alternative solutions in light of consequences.

*Dan asked Greg for permission to draw on the bottom part and promised him that next time, when Dan has the board, he'll share it with Greg. This solution satisfied both children, and any potential teacher-child power play was averted.*

**Situation 3:** Kim is interfering with a game of jump rope by pushing Marta, who is jumping, aside.

Teacher: Why are you interfering with their game?

Kim: They won't let me jump.

Teacher: How do you know that?[1]

Kim: 'Cause they told me to go away.

Teacher: Breaking up their game is *one* thing you can do. What happened when you did that?[2]

Kim: Marta screamed at me.

Teacher: How did that make you feel?[3]

Kim: Frustrated.

Teacher: Can you think of a DIFFERENT way to solve this problem so Marta won't scream and you won't feel frustrated?[4]

Kim: I could ask them again, but they'll say no.

Teacher: They might say no. What else can you think of?[5]

Kim: I can show them how to double jump.

Teacher: Which of those ideas do you like better?[6]

Kim: Show them how to double jump. They'll want me to teach them how.

Teacher: You really thought this problem through now. Go ahead and try that.

## NOTES

[1] Guides thinking to help the child avoid false conclusions.

[2] Asks the child to identify consequences.

[3] Guides thinking about the child's own feelings in light of consequences.

[4] Encourages thinking of alternative solutions.

[5] Guides the child not to give up too soon.

[6] Guides the child to consider the best option.

**Situation 4:** Shawn accuses Lamont of stealing his quarter. The teacher has reason to believe this may be true.

Teacher: *(Privately, to Lamont)* Shawn is upset because he thinks you took his quarter at recess when it fell out of his pocket.

Lamont: No, I didn't!

Teacher: If you did or didn't, if you tell me what happened, I can try to help.[1]

Lamont: We were just playing, and he got mad.

Teacher: *(Very casually)* I see, so you were playing.

Lamont: Well, his quarter dropped, and I found it. So it's mine.

Teacher: Do you think you and Shawn feel the SAME way about that?[2]

Lamont: I don't care. It's mine!

Teacher: How might you feel if *you* dropped your money and someone found it and kept it?[2]

Lamont: I guess I'd be mad.

Teacher: Can you think of a way to solve this problem?[3]

Lamont: *(Thinks a moment)* I can keep it 'cause it's mine.

*At this point, the teacher persuaded Lamont to return the quarter. Importantly, this was the first time that Lamont, who frequently took things from other children, openly admitted it. Later, when emotions subsided, the teacher followed up on the situation with Shawn and the rest of the class:*

Teacher: Shawn, can you think of a way to keep your money from falling out of your pocket at recess?

Shawn: I can tape it in.

Teacher: That's *one* way. Can you think of a DIFFERENT way?

Shawn: No.

Teacher: *(To the class)* Can anyone help us?[4]

Child 1: He can give it to you to keep when he goes out to recess.

Child 2: He can spend it before recess.

Lamont: He can hide it.[5]

Teacher: *(To Shawn)* OK. We have three DIFFERENT ideas here. Which one do you like best? Why?

*Involving Lamont in the thinking process may have been an important contribution toward his improved behavior over the course of the school year. Although the teacher did have to persuade Lamont to return the quarter this time, consistent problem-solving dialoguing helped him recognize that he would have more friends by increasing his positive interactions with his peers.*

## NOTES

[1] Seeks child's view of the problem.

[2] Guides child to see his own and other's point of view.

[3] Encourages child to think of his own solution.

[4] Asks other children to help think the problem through, rather than giving suggestions.

[5] Lamont is free to enter the situation without the teacher's having to refer to his taking the quarter.

## TEACHER-CHILD PROBLEMS

**Situation 1:** Felicia feels the teacher is unfair to her.

Felicia:   You never pick me to be the messenger.

Teacher:   Do you know why?

Felicia:   No. It's not fair.

Teacher:   What happened last time I sent you with a message to take to the office?

Felicia:   Oh . . . I messed around in the halls.

Teacher:   How do I feel about that?

Felicia:   Mad.

Teacher:   What do you suggest I do about this?

Felicia:   Give me another chance.

Teacher:   OK. We'll try this one more time.

*Before ICPS training, this teacher might have said, "Last time I sent you out, you were caught messing around, and that's not what I sent you to do." After ICPS training, the teacher guided the child to think about what she did. The teacher accepted the solution Felicia offered, keeping the lines of communication open.*

*Not all problems end up with the child's obtaining his or her wish, however. There are some outcomes about which the child has no choice. In the context of ICPS, the child can be helped to think about why a wish cannot be fulfilled.*

**Situation 2:** Anton, against his teacher's established rules, is chewing gum in class.

Teacher: Anton, do you know the rule about chewing gum in class?

Anton: Yeah. *(Keeps chewing.)*

Teacher: Why do you think we have that rule?

Anton: 'Cause it bothers you.

Teacher: That's *one* reason. Why else do you think we have that rule?

Anton: I don't know.

Teacher: Can anybody help us?

Child 1: If he can chew gum, so can we.

Child 2: And he might leave it on his seat, and someone might sit on it.

Anton: I won't do that. Really, I won't.

Teacher: Yes, that's probably true, Anton. What might the rest of the class think if I let you chew gum?

Anton: That it's OK to chew gum.

Teacher: What would it sound like if everyone chewed gum at the SAME TIME?

Anton: It would be too noisy.

Teacher: Is it fair for you to chew gum and not the others?

Anton: No. *(Puts his gum in the wastebasket.)*

*Before ICPS training, this teacher might have explained why she imposed the rule, a technique more effective than simple demands but one that still does the thinking for the child. ICPS dialoguing defuses any potential defiance from Anton.*

# What Might Happen Next, Part II

## PURPOSE

To further promote children's understanding of consequences and evaluation of solutions

## MATERIALS

Chalkboard or easel

## TEACHER SCRIPT

Today we're going to play a team game, and we'll divide the class into two teams.

*Divide the class into Team A and Team B.*

First I'll tell you a problem.

After you give me a few solutions, we'll pick one of them.

The idea of the game is to think of lots of DIFFERENT consequences, things that might happen next.

Here's the problem: Joseph wants Evan to let him try his picture puzzle.

Evan won't let Joseph try his puzzle.

*Elicit solutions and write them on the chalkboard in the usual way. Pick one or let the group pick one—for example, "Grab some pieces of the puzzle." Next write the following questions on the chalkboard:*

What might Joseph *do?*

What might Joseph *say?*

How might Joseph *feel?*

*(To Team A)* OK. Here's how we'll play the game.

First _____, tell us a consequence if Joseph grabs some pieces of the puzzle. *(Name the first child on Team A.)*

273

It can be something Evan might do, say, or feel.

*If the response is relevant:* That's *one* thing that might happen next.

*If the response is not relevant:* Why might that happen?

*If the consequence is relevant, write it on the chalkboard under a heading for Team A, as the example shows.*

> (*To the first member of Team B*) Now, _____, tell us a DIFFERENT consequence.
>
> (*If relevant*) That's a DIFFERENT consequence.

*Write this consequence on the chalkboard under a heading for Team B, as the example shows.*

> OK, everybody, watch for *enumerations*—you know, consequences that are kind of the SAME.
>
> If you catch any, let us know.

*If there is disagreement about an enumeration, discuss. If the group decides a response is an enumeration, give the child who caught it a chance to offer a different consequence. Continue to give the teams alternate chances to think of different consequences.*

*Classify enumerations and give check marks for original consequences, as in Lesson 42.*

*Some possible responses and their classification are shown in the following example.*

| **Team A** | **Team B** |
|---|---|
| ✓(A) 1. He'll say, "I won't be your friend anymore." | ✓(B) 1. He'll tell his father. |
| (B) 2. He'll tell his mother. | ✓(E) 2. He won't let Joseph have anything of his anymore. |
| ✓ C 3. He'll say, "Give that back!" | (E) 3. He won't share with Joseph. |
| (A) 4. He won't play with Joseph anymore. | ✓ F 4. He'll be mad. |
| ✓ D 5. He'll grab the pieces back. | ✓ G 5. They'll fight. |
| Total for Team A: 3 (Numbers 1, 3, and 5) | Total for Team B: 4 (Numbers 1, 2, 4, and 5) |

*Across and within teams, the same circled letters are enumerations; the ones with check marks are original solutions.*

*In this example, Team A has three different consequences; Team B has four. Because Team B gave the response "He'll tell his father" before Team B gave the response "He'll tell his mother," Team B gets credit for the consequence.*

---

**HINT**

If a child becomes disruptive, you can intervene with this same kind of inquiry. For example, you might say, "Anita, why are you bothering your neighbor? What might happen if you keep bothering her? How might she feel? Can you think of something DIFFERENT you can do so that won't happen?"

You could approach inattentive behavior by saying, for example, "Raymond is reading a book. We are talking about consequences. Are Raymond and the rest of us doing the SAME thing or something DIFFERENT?"

---

# What Might Happen Next, Part III

## PURPOSE

To further promote children's understanding of consequences and evaluation of solutions

## MATERIALS

Chalkboard or easel

Paper and pencils

## TEACHER SCRIPT

Today we're going to divide up into small groups to think about consequences—what might happen next if someone does or says something.

But first I'll tell you a problem and you give me some solutions. The problem is that Marie just got a part in the school play.

She wants Olivia to help her make posters so all the kids will know about the play.

Tell me all the things Marie can say or do to get Olivia to help her make the posters.

*Generate alternative solutions and write them on the chalkboard in the usual way. Pick or have the group vote on one solution from the list to discuss, then divide the class into groups of about six children each.*

*For this problem, the response "Marie can make her own posters" is irrelevant as a solution because the problem is not how to get the posters made, but how to get Olivia to help make them. If a child proposes this as a solution, you might say, "Yes, Marie could make her own. Remember, the problem is that she wants to think of ways to get Marie to help her."*

*(To the groups)* Try to think of DIFFERENT things that might happen next if _____. *(Repeat the chosen solution.)*

Here are some things to think about. *(Write the following list of questions on the board.)*

What might happen next?

What might Marie *do?*

What might Marie *say?*

How might Marie *feel?*

*Pick a team captain to write down each group's consequences. When the groups have finished their discussion, have the first team captain present that group's consequences to the class. Record the first group's consequences on the board, then ask the whole class:*

Does anyone see any enumerations—you know, consequences that are kind of the SAME?

*If yes:* How are these consequences the SAME?

*Here, enumerations are noted within the small groups, not between teams, as in Lessons 42 and 49. Continue until all enumerations are accounted for and classified, pointing out any the children do not catch.*

*If a consequence is unclear or appears irrelevant, say, "Tell us more about that" or ask, "Why might that happen next?" Then count the number of different, relevant consequences and put that number on the board.*

*Repeat this process for each of the remaining groups. Make sure the consequences given by each group are their own alone, not copied from other groups after discussion.*

*If you cannot do all the small groups in one day, collect their papers, note the team members' names, and continue another time.*

# Consequential Thinking

**MATH**

*Children can use bar graphs to illustrate the number of consequences they generate in Lesson 50. The following example shows how one set of responses might be graphed.*

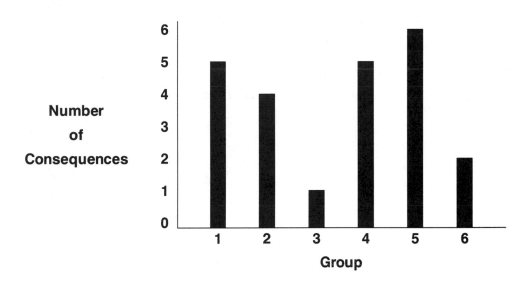

Which group had the greatest number of consequences?

Did any groups have the SAME number of consequences?

What is the mean number of consequences given by ALL of the groups?

Who can think of a DIFFERENT way to draw the SAME information?

*For example:*

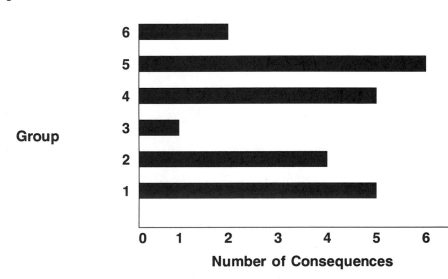

## SOCIAL STUDIES

What might have happened if . . .

- George Washington's soldiers did not listen to him during the crossing of the Delaware?
- Martin Luther King had not been assassinated?
- Robert Kennedy had not been assassinated?
- The King of England had not taxed the colonists so much before 1776?
- Columbus had not reached America in 1492?
- Automobiles were never invented?
- Cities had no governments?
- Your parents weren't allowed to vote their choice for President?

*Let the group make up their own examples.*


## SCIENCE

What might happen if . . .

- You put two cans of fish food in an aquarium?
- You leave meat out of the refrigerator for 3 days?
- You leave a cover on a pot of boiling water for an hour?
- You eat potato chips and candy all day?
- You leave ice out of the freezer for a couple of hours?
- People keep throwing garbage into lakes, rivers, and oceans?
- Someone smokes cigarettes?
- Someone uses drugs or drinks alcohol?

*Let the group make up other examples.*

# Pros and Cons

*Use anything your class is studying to help them consider pros and cons. For example:*

- The 13 colonies' declaration of independence from England
- Native Americans' "selling" their land to the English settlers
- Puerto Rico's becoming the fifty-first state
- The Baltic States' becoming independent from the Soviet Union
- The United States' deciding to go to war against Iraq in 1991
- The limiting of time a United States President may serve to two terms

*You may wish to let the children make up their own statements of this kind, possibly as a homework assignment.*

# What Makes People Act the Way They Do?

**PURPOSE**

To encourage appreciation of the reasons behind what people do

**MATERIALS**

None

**TEACHER SCRIPT**

---

**NOTE**

The situations described in this lesson use letters instead of names to designate characters. If one child mentions another child by name during the lesson, say, "Let's not talk about real people—just why someone might do this."

---

We all know that some people do things over and over, even though they know the consequences might not be good ones.

But we often don't stop to think about why these people keep doing these things so much.

I'm going to tell you some things kids do, and you think of lots of DIFFERENT possible reasons why they might keep doing them.

OK, here's the first one.

**Situation 1:** A keeps working on his math lessons too fast, and he makes lots of mistakes. His teachers tell him that he would do better if he'd work slower, but he keeps rushing anyway.

Why does A keep rushing through his math?

How does the fact that *(repeat reason given)* make him keep on doing this? (*For example:* How does his not liking math make him keep on rushing through?)

Can anyone think of a DIFFERENT reason A keeps doing this?

How does the fact that _____ make him keep on doing this? (*Repeat the second answer given. For example:* "He wants to be the first one finished.")

*Elicit additional reasons. After all have been given:*

> If the reason is _____, how can we help A stop rushing through his work and making lots of mistakes?
> *(Repeat one reason given.)*
>
> Would we help a DIFFERENT way if we know that _____?
> *(Repeat another reason given.)*
>
> Is there anything else anyone wants to say about this situation?

> **Situation 2:** B keeps teasing her classmates. The kids keep telling her she'll lose all her friends if she keeps doing that, but she keeps on teasing anyway.

*Repeat the same line of questioning as for Situation 1. If children get side-tracked by the content of the teasing (for example, "She calls people stupid"), help them focus on the reason for the teasing instead (for example, to get attention).*

> **Situation 3:** C is always getting ANGRY for no good reason—you know, flies off the handle at little things. Everyone tells him they don't like that, but he keeps on getting ANGRY anyway.

*Repeat the same line of questioning as for Situation 1.*

> **Situation 4:** D is very shy and is scared to play with other kids. She stands around and watches them play but never joins in.

*Repeat the same line of questioning as for Situation 1, then ask the group if they can think of any other things people do that could be talked about in this way. Discuss as time and interest permit.*

---

**HINT**

After each situation is presented, it is OK if children who actually engage in the behavior described volunteer information about themselves. You may even wish to ask, "Does anyone who really does this want to tell us why you think you do?"

---

# How Does Each Person See the Problem?

## PURPOSE

To help children use previously learned skills of consequential thinking to practice decision making

## MATERIALS

Chalkboard or easel

Illustrations 21 and 22

## TEACHER SCRIPT

*Show children Illustration 21.*

What problem do you see in this picture?

What might each person in the picture be thinking and feeling?

Who should try to solve this problem? *(Repeat the problem named.)*

What can this person do or say to solve the problem?

*Elicit as many alternative solutions as possible, writing each on the chalkboard in the usual way. Classify enumerations and clarify seemingly irrelevant responses.*

Which solution do you think is the best one?

Why do you think that one is the best?

*Focus on why that solution is the best one, not why another solution is not. If, for example, a child says, "Asking is better than pushing because if she pushes, the other girl might knock her down," you might respond, "OK, if pushing is NOT a good solution, why IS asking a good one?"*

Does anyone think a solution not already on our list is the best one?

Why?

Is there anyone else in this picture who could help solve this problem?

How?

Who sees a DIFFERENT problem?

*Let children name as many different problems as they can.*

DIFFERENT people can see the SAME thing and think DIFFERENT things are happening.

If these were real people, how could you find out what the problem really is? (*If needed:* Ask.)

Can you think of a time when you had a problem and felt FRUSTRATED because someone misunderstood what your problem was?

What about a time when you misunderstood what someone else's problem was?

*Repeat this line of questioning for Illustration 22.*

ILLUSTRATION 21  Lesson 52

ILLUSTRATION 22   Lesson 52

# Pick the Best, Pick the Worst

## PURPOSE

To help children practice making decisions by picking the best and worst solutions, based on potential consequences

## MATERIALS

Chalkboard or easel

## TEACHER SCRIPT

Today we're going to talk about a problem that comes up a lot in real life.

After you tell me lots of solutions, we're going to do something a little DIFFERENT with them.

The problem is that Angela wants to borrow Steven's pencil, but Steven might not let her.

What can Angela do or say so she can end up using Steven's pencil?

*Elicit alternative solutions in the usual way, writing each on the chalkboard. Clarify seemingly irrelevant responses; classify enumerations. After a number of solutions have been generated, read different, relevant solutions aloud. Next group the enumerations together on the board as shown in the example.*

| Category | Enumerations |
| --- | --- |
| Asking | Ask him politely. |
| | Ask him nicely. |
| | Say please. |
| | |
| Returning a favor | Say, "You can use my pen." |
| | Say, "I'll let you use mine when you need it." |
| | |
| Bargaining friendship | Say, "I'll be your friend." |
| | Say, "I won't be your friend." |
| | |
| Attacking | Hit him. |
| | Fight him. |
| | Kick him. |
| | |
| Snatching | Take it. |
| | Grab it. |
| | Snatch it. |
| | |
| Sneaking | Steal it. |
| | Take it when he's not looking. |
| | Hide it. |
| | |
| Lending | Say, "I'll give it right back." |
| | Say, "I'll only use it a little while." |

*Read the list of solutions given to the problem. Treat enumerations as one—for example, say, "He could ask him politely, ask him nicely, say please—all forms of asking—OR he could _____."*

> *(To a specific child)* Which solution do you think is best?
>
> Why?
>
> Which solution do you think is worst?
>
> Why?

*If the child says, for example, that asking is best because if Angela hits, she'll get hit back, he or she is really answering the question of why hitting is worst. Say to the child, "That might happen. Why is asking best? Why do you like that better?"*

> *(To the group)* Who has a DIFFERENT opinion about which solution is best and why?
>
> Who has a DIFFERENT opinion about which solution is worst and why?

*Continue asking for different opinions as long as time and interest permit.*

*Encourage children to discuss the effect of a particular solution on others, including others' feelings. Another, more difficult question you may wish to ask is "What might Angela know about how Steven thinks and feels that could help her find the best solution?"*

## OPTION

> On the same or a different day, let children pick a solution. Have one child act out the solution and another child respond to it. Let these two actors role-play until the one child lets the other use his or her pencil. If time and interest permit, two different actors can role-play a different solution.

# SOLUTION-CONSEQUENCE PAIRS

The lessons in this section help teach children how to generate solution-consequence pairs. By doing so, children will ultimately be able to choose from among a number of solutions on the basis of their most likely consequences: "If I do this, *that* might happen; if I do that, *this* might happen."

## PROCEDURE

As shown in the lessons, the steps for teaching solution-consequence pairs are as follows:

1. State the problem or have the child state the problem.
2. Elicit one solution to the problem.
3. Ask for a consequence of that solution.
4. If the consequence is relevant, elicit a second solution.
5. Ask for the consequence of the second solution, and so on, as the example shows.

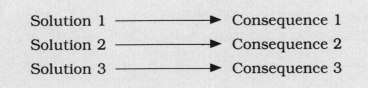

Solution 1 ⟶ Consequence 1

Solution 2 ⟶ Consequence 2

Solution 3 ⟶ Consequence 3

## ENUMERATIONS AND UNCLEAR OR APPARENTLY IRRELEVANT RESPONSES

Treat enumerations and apparently irrelevant responses as you would for alternative solutions or consequences. Distinguish chain reactions from consequences if necessary.

# What Can I Do? Is That a Good Idea?

## PURPOSE

To encourage solution-consequence pairing as a way of encouraging immediate evaluation of solutions in light of consequences

## MATERIALS

Illustrations 23–27

## TEACHER SCRIPT

*Place Illustrations 23–27 on the ledge of a chalkboard, turned around so that the blank side is facing the class. You can either mount the pictures on posterboard so they will stand up or tape them so they will stay in place.*

Today we are going to talk about solutions and consequences in a new way—*solution-consequence pairs.*

That's when you give a solution and then its consequence right away.

*Divide the group into two teams of five to seven children each.*

(*To a child on Team A*) Pick any picture, then show it to your team and the other team.

Name a problem between people that you think this picture shows. (*If the child does not name an interpersonal problem:* What problem do you see that could be between people?)

What might have led up to (caused) the problem?

How is each person in the picture feeling?

*Ask different children on Team A to answer the following questions:*

What can the person with the problem do or say to solve the problem?

What might happen next if (he/she) does that?

What might the other person do or say?

*Write the solution and its immediate consequence on the chalkboard under a heading for Team A, as shown in the example. Draw an arrow from solution to consequence.*

**Team A**

Solution 1 ──▶ Consequence 1

*Next direct the same questions to members of Team B.*

> What else could the person in this picture do or say to solve this problem?
>
> What might happen next if (he/she) does that?
>
> What might the other person do or say?

*Write this solution and its immediate consequence under a heading for Team B, as shown in the example. Draw an arrow from solution to consequence.*

**Team A**

Solution 1 ──▶ Consequence 1

**Team B**

Solution 1 ──▶ Consequence 1

> OK, now we're going to switch back and forth from Team A to Team B.
>
> Each team will give one new and DIFFERENT solution and a consequence for that solution.
>
> That is a solution-consequence pair.
>
> Listen for solutions that are enumerations—kind of the SAME as one already given by either team.
>
> Someone who catches an enumeration can have a chance to give a DIFFERENT solution.

*When no one on the last team to respond can give a new, different solution, the other team gets a chance. If someone on the other team can give one, and can give a consequence pair, that team wins the game by having the greatest number of solution-consequence pairs.*

*After the children run out of solution-consequence pairs, ask:*

> How might the person who has the problem feel before
> (his/her) problem is solved?

> How might that person feel after (his/her) problem is solved?

*Use this procedure on the same or a different day with remaining pictures, each with a new team. Let a new child choose a picture each time.*

## OPTIONS

1. Have the entire group generate as many solution-consequence pairs as possible, without making the procedure a team game. You can still allow a child to select the illustration.

2. Divide the class into small groups and give each group one illustration. Have each group describe a problem and generate as many solution-consequence pairs as possible. When finished, the groups may present their problem and solution-consequence pairs to the class.

ILLUSTRATION 23   Lesson 54

ILLUSTRATION 24  Lesson 54

ILLUSTRATION 25   Lesson 54

ILLUSTRATION 26   Lesson 54

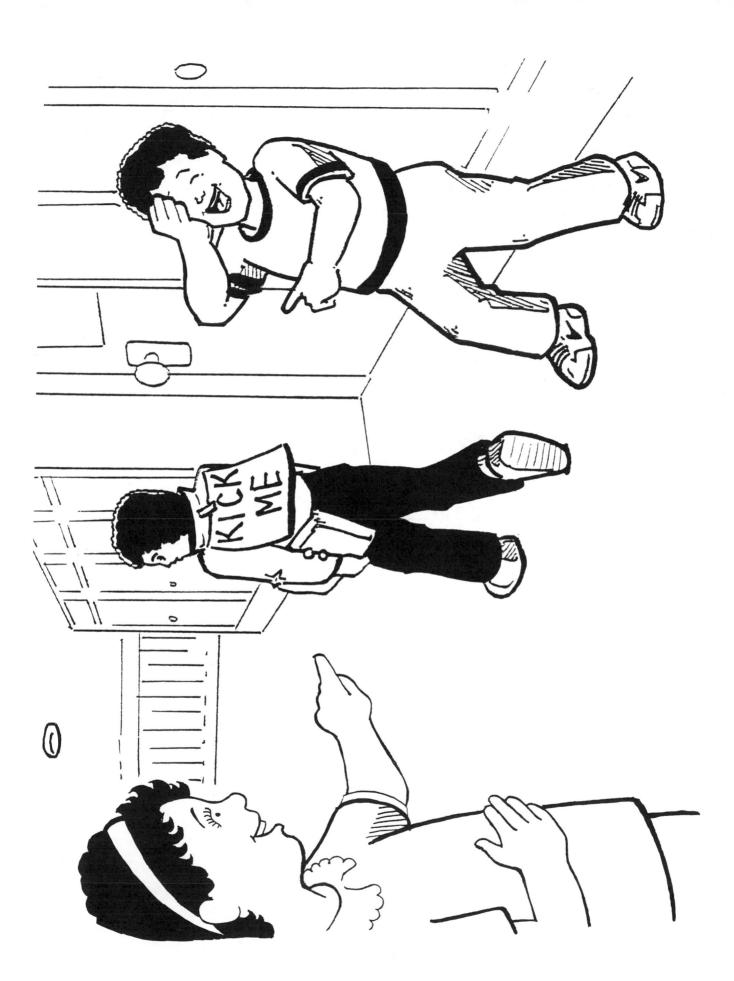

ILLUSTRATION 27   Lesson 54

# Role-Playing, Part III

## PURPOSE

To provide more practice in problem solving and immediate evaluation of solutions in light of consequences

## MATERIALS

Illustrations 23–27 (from Lesson 54)

Any hand puppets (optional)

Paper and pencils

## TEACHER SCRIPT

*Display Illustrations 23–27 so the whole group can see them. Pick a child to choose one problem to role-play from those depicted in the illustrations. Then let that child pick as many more children as needed to role-play the problem. Children may use puppets if they wish.*

(To the actors) When you plan your role-play, be sure the person solving the problem has to try more than one solution.

The other(s) will show us what will happen next—or what they'll do or say.

(To the rest of the group, while the actors are planning their role-play) Choose one of the problems we talked about before, or make up a new one.

Write a role-play using the characters you need to solve the problem.

After you have a character in your play try a solution, write the next thing that happens—maybe what the other character(s) will do or say.

Be sure to use more than one way, more than one solution in your role-play.

*Before the role-players act out their scene:*

> OK, now the actors will do their role-play.
>
> Listen carefully to the solutions and consequences
> (what happens next, what the other does or says) and
> remember them because I'm going to ask you about them
> when the role-play is finished.

*Have the role-players act out their scene.*

> OK. Who remembers one solution the problem solver tried
> and what the consequence was—that is, what happened next?

*Repeat until children have identified all the solution-consequence pairs.*

> Can anyone think of something else the problem solver
> could have tried?
>
> What might the consequence of that be?

*As time and interest permit, let other children perform their role-plays for the class. This may be continued on a different day, if desired.*

# Solution-Consequence Pairs

## ROLE-PLAYING REAL PROBLEMS

*When actual problems arise in the gym, at recess, at lunchtime, and so forth, let those involved meet in the hallway or in the corner of the room and create a role-play. Tell them to include:*

- What happened (the problem)
- How each person feels (or felt)
- Several solutions to the problem and their consequences, with comments on whether a solution is or is not a good one

*Others in the class can add alternative solutions when the role-play is performed.*

## WRITING DOWN REAL PROBLEMS

*Encourage children to think of a problem they experienced, a solution they actually tried, and its consequence. These can be written on 3 × 5–inch cards and displayed on a bulletin board in the classroom or in the halls.*

*Children can also write, for a school newsletter, the problems they experience and how they solved them.*

# Is That My First Idea?

## PURPOSE

To help children appreciate that problems cannot always be solved quickly and that the first idea one thinks of may not always be the best one

To give children a chance to think further about choice of solutions in light of consequences

## MATERIALS

Activity Sheet 16

## TEACHER SCRIPT

*Give each child a copy of Activity Sheet 16.*

Before, we used cartoon balloons to fill in what someone was thinking about a feeling word.

Now we'll use cartoon balloons in a new way.

We're going to use the balloons to help the stick-figure character think of solutions to a people problem.

The balloon that says Solution 1, right above the stick figure, is for the first idea that comes to your mind. *(Point.)*

The balloon above that is for your second idea *(point)*, above that for your third *(point)*, and so on.

*Make sure the class understands this idea before proceeding.*

Here's the problem: A went to pick up B to go to the movies, but B wasn't ready on time.

B made A miss the first part of the movie because they got there late.

Now A is ANGRY at B.

B is the stick figure and has to solve this problem.

What can B do or say so A won't be ANGRY?

In the balloon labeled Solution 1, write the first idea that comes to your mind, very quickly. *(Allow only 5 seconds.)*

OK, now take more time to think of a second solution.

Write that in the balloon that says Solution 2.
*(Give the group a minute or two.)*

Now think of three more solutions, one for each of the rest
of the balloons.

Try to think of DIFFERENT ideas, not enumerations.
*(Give the group a few more minutes.)*

Now you're going to decide how good you think each solution is.

On the line to the right of each balloon *(point)*, put two stars
if you think the solution in that balloon is very good.

If you think a solution is sort of OK, put one star on the line.

If you think a solution is not good at all, put a zero on the
line next to that balloon.

You don't have to use all three symbols—that is, you don't have
to put a zero next to any of them if you think all of your solutions
are very good or sort of OK.

Just put whatever symbol you think each solution should be.

OK, take a few minutes and put your thoughts of how good
each solution is on the line next to the balloon.

*(When children have finished)* If you thought your first solution
was not good at all—zero—raise your hand.

Raise your hand if you thought your first idea was one star,
sort of OK.

Raise your hand if you thought your first idea was two stars,
very good.

Raise your hand if your first idea was either a zero or one star AND a
solution in any balloon after that—NOT your first idea—was two stars.

*(Regardless of how children respond)* Sometimes it takes time
to think, and the first idea that pops into your head is not always
the best thing to do.

OK, now I'll call on one of you to read all five of your solutions.

The rest of you listen carefully and see if you had the SAME one
or one like it.

*Call on someone likely to have five different solutions.*

Now I'm going to ask _____ to tell us how good (he/she) thinks
each solution is.

The rest of you listen carefully.

If you have the SAME solution or one like it, see if you agree
or do NOT agree about how good it is.

*(To the child)* Did any of your solutions get a zero?

*If yes:* Which one?

Why do you think that solution is NOT a good idea?
*(Repeat for each solution rated zero.)*

*Repeat this line of questioning for one-star and two-star solutions.*

Is there anything else you'd like to say about your solutions?

*(To the group)* Did _____ have any enumerations?
*(If yes, discuss.)*

If anyone had the SAME solution as any you just heard,
or one like it, raise your hand.

*(To any children who respond)* Did you give that solution
a zero, one star, or two stars?

Did _____ give that solution the SAME number of stars
or a DIFFERENT number?

*If the same:* OK, you both feel the SAME way about the
SAME solution.

*If different:* Oh, you and _____ feel a DIFFERENT way
about the SAME solution.

Why do you feel the solution is *(repeat rating)*?

*Call on others who had the same solution(s) and repeat this line of questioning.*

Who had a solution that we have not heard yet?

What did you give it? A zero, one star, or two stars?

Did anyone else have the SAME idea?

How did you rate it?

Is that the SAME or DIFFERENT from what the other person gave it?

*Repeat with other children as time and interest permit.*

---

**HINT**

Do not reveal your own feelings about any of the solutions. Instead,
stress the *process* of thinking about and evaluating solutions.

---

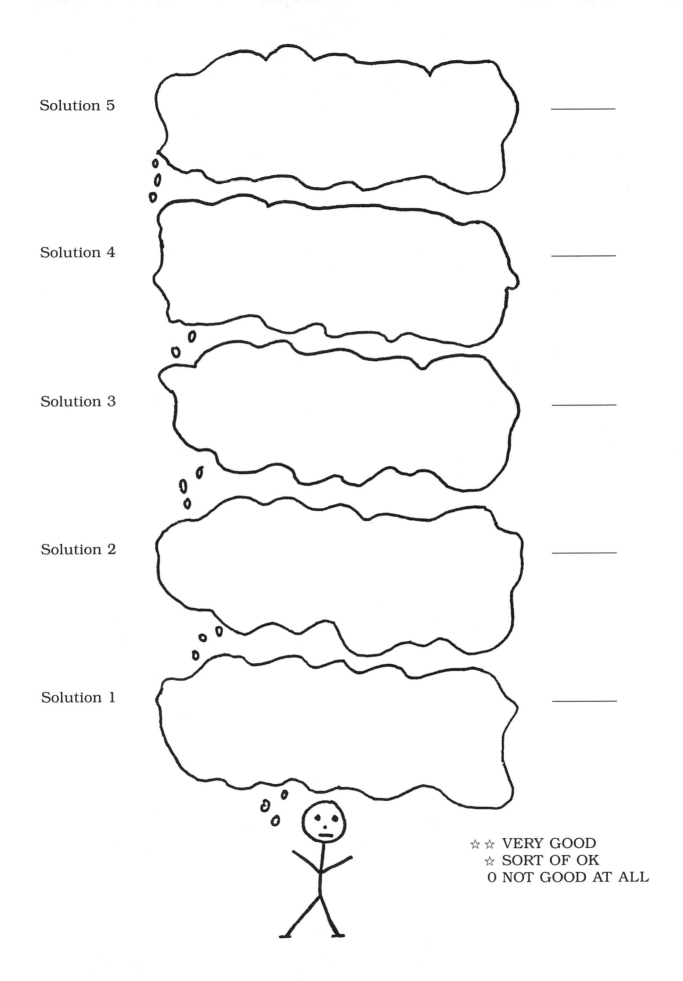

Solution 5

Solution 4

Solution 3

Solution 2

Solution 1

☆ ☆ VERY GOOD
☆ SORT OF OK
0 NOT GOOD AT ALL

ACTIVITY SHEET 16  Lesson 56

# Did I ICPS Today?

## PURPOSE

To help children practice the use of ICPS dialoguing techniques

## MATERIALS

Activity Sheet 17

## TEACHER SCRIPT

1. Ask children to remember a problem they really had with a friend, classmate, parent, teacher—anyone. For this lesson, children may make up a problem if they cannot think of an actual one at the moment.

2. Have each child fill out a copy of Activity Sheet 17 to describe the event.

3. Discuss any problems the children are willing to share.

4. Tell children that a pile of "Did I ICPS Today" sheets will be available on your desk (or at some other permanent location) and that whenever they have a problem with someone they may fill out one of these sheets.

---

**HINT**

Offer the sheets as an option for children, not as an assignment that must be completed for every problem that comes up. Some children will feel comfortable reading their responses on these sheets aloud and discussing them with the class. Others will prefer to have written comments from you or to keep the sheets in a private ICPS diary. Because the purpose of these sheets is to guide ICPS thinking, any of these options is acceptable.

---

# DID I ICPS TODAY?

1. The problem was _____

   _____

2. Who was involved? _____ and _____ and _____

3. Before the problem was solved, I felt _____ and _____

4. The other person (or people) felt _____ and _____

5. I did or said (my solution) _____

   _____

6. What happened next (the consequence) was _____

   _____

7. Was the problem solved? _____

8. If the problem was not solved, I could have tried a different way. Five things I could have done or said are:

   a. _____

   b. _____

   c. _____

   d. _____

   e. _____

9. Which one might be the best solution of all? _____

10. Why might that solution be the best one? _____

    _____

11. Some things I might think about the next time a problem comes up are _____

    _____

    _____

# Good Times and Not Good Times to Act

## PURPOSE

To introduce the idea of timing, a precursor to planning, or means-ends thinking, in problem solving

## MATERIALS

Paper and pencils

## TEACHER SCRIPT

Good problem solvers think about a lot of things when they have a problem that involves other people.

One of these things is *when* to do something.

I'm going to tell you some things kids did and when they did it.

*Ask children to take out paper and pencils and number a page from 1 to 10.*

If the kid I tell you about did what he or she did at a GOOD TIME, write the letter G next to the number.

If the kid did it at a NOT GOOD TIME, write the letters NG next to the number.

OK. Write G for a GOOD TIME and NG for a NOT GOOD TIME.

*Change the names in the following examples if they are the same as those of children in your class.*

1. John asks his friend Karl to play basketball with him—just after Karl breaks his leg.
2. Raymond asks his brother to help him with his homework— while his brother is coming down from an airplane in a parachute.
3. Ruth wins 100 dollars and tells her friend—at 3 o'clock in the morning.
4. Susan asks her mother for a new dress—right before Susan's birthday.
5. Tommy asks his teacher something—while his teacher is talking to the principal at the door.

6. Ralph asks his teacher for a drink of water—just when everyone is quiet and ready to start a test.

7. Robert asks William for a turn with the marbles—right after William finishes with his turn.

8. Barbara asks Carol if she can borrow a pencil—right after Carol is scolded by her teacher.

9. Steven asks Terry for a favor—while Terry is screaming in pain after falling off his bike.

10. Natasha asks her mother for a new bike—just after Natasha carelessly leaves her old bike out on the street and it gets stolen.

*Read each item one at a time and say:*

Who said *G* for a GOOD TIME to do that? Raise your hand.

Who said *NG* for a NOT GOOD TIME to do that?

(*If there is any disagreement:* Can you tell us why you think that?)

*Choose three or four of the examples of not good times and let a few children tell why they are not good and when a good time would be. Encourage children to make up their own examples of good and not good times.*

# What Can I Do While I Wait?

## PURPOSE

To help children cope with frustration when their immediate needs cannot be satisfied

## MATERIALS

Paper and pencils

## TEACHER SCRIPT

Sometimes people want something, but they can't always have it when they want it—or they might want to do something with someone, but that person is busy.

The game for today is called What Can I Do While I Wait?

I'm going to tell you some things that kids might want to have or do, but they can't have them or do them right away.

*Ask children to take out paper and pencils.*

You write down five DIFFERENT things you could do if you were the kid I'm going to tell about.

Here's the first one.

*Be sure to change the names of the children in the examples if they are the same as those of children in the class.*

1. The scene is the playground after school. Roscoe wants to fly Peter's model airplane, and Peter says Roscoe can when Peter finishes flying it first. Write down five things Roscoe can do while he waits.

2. Deborah wants her mother to help her with her violin lesson, but her mother has to finish reading a story to Deborah's 3-year-old sister. Write down five things Deborah could do while she waits.

3. Think of a time you had to wait for something and NOT be IMPATIENT. Write down where you were. Now write down five things you could have done while you waited.

*As time and interest permit, let children read their answers. Ask if anyone thought of something different they could do.*

# Is This a Good Time to Act?

## PURPOSE

To develop further sensitivity to timing as an important element in problem solving

## MATERIALS

Illustrations 28 and 29

## TEACHER SCRIPT

Let's talk some more about GOOD TIMES and NOT GOOD TIMES to do things.

*Show children Illustration 28.*

What is happening in this picture?

Is this a GOOD TIME or a NOT GOOD TIME for this girl to talk to her mother?

Why do you think that? (*If needed:* Can the mother talk to the girl AND the baby at the SAME TIME? How will the mother feel if the girl tries to talk to her now?)

Does anyone have a DIFFERENT thought about this?

Why do you think about it that way?

If you think this is a NOT GOOD TIME, what can this girl do while she waits?

What else can she do?

*Repeat this line of questioning for Illustration 29. If needed, ask, "Can the mother talk to the boy AND be on the phone at the SAME TIME?"*

Picking GOOD TIMES is part of *planning* to reach a goal.

Can you think of a GOOD TIME to do something?

What about a NOT GOOD TIME?

*Let children name as many examples as time and interest permit.*

ILLUSTRATION 28  Lesson 60

ILLUSTRATION 29  Lesson 60

# When Is a Good Time to Act?

## PURPOSE

To develop further sensitivity to timing as an important element in problem solving

## MATERIALS

Any three hand puppets (optional)

## TEACHER SCRIPT

*Act out the following scenes, using different voices for the various puppets. If puppets are not available, you can use paper bags or socks, let children make their own puppets, or ask two children to take the parts of Ollie and Tippy.*

Teacher: I'm a teacher, and the kids in my class are really going at it today. I feel ANGRY and FRUSTRATED.

Ollie: Ms. Smith, can I go to my brother's room to give him my football?

Teacher: No, Ollie! I'm very ANGRY, and I can't deal with that right now.

Ollie: *(Moves away, looking sad and frustrated.)* OK. Now watch and listen. It's a little later, and Ms. Smith is feeling better. She is not ANGRY now.

*Place another puppet in your hand.*

Teacher: *(With a happy or neutral expression)*

Tippy: Ms. Smith, can I go to my brother's room to give him my football?

Teacher: If you are finished with your math, you may go.

Who picked a better time to tell a problem to the teacher, Ollie or Tippy?

Why?

Can the SAME person feel DIFFERENT ways at DIFFERENT times?

Who felt a DIFFERENT way at a DIFFERENT time in this story?

Let's talk some more about *your* questions and NOT GOOD TIMES.

Think of someone—a mother, father, sister, brother, friend, anyone.

Can you think of a time it was better to wait for what you wanted?

What could you have done while you waited?

Sometimes you can wait too long: You can't wait until *after* your mother has gone to the store to tell her what you'd like her to bring you.

Can you think of a time you waited too long?

# A Good/Not Good Time, What Can I Do While I Wait?

## SOME HELPFUL QUESTIONS

### When a child interrupts:

Can I talk to you AND to _____ at the SAME TIME?

If you talk to me while I'm talking with someone else, how will I probably feel?

If I am talking to someone, is that a GOOD TIME or a NOT GOOD TIME to talk to me?

When is a GOOD TIME?

Can you think of something DIFFERENT to do while you wait?

### When a child shouts out:

If I did NOT call on you and you know the answer, I understand you feel _____. *(Let the child respond.)*

But I can NOT call on two people at the SAME TIME.

If you shout out an answer when I call on someone else, is that a GOOD TIME or a NOT GOOD TIME?

### When a child is talking to others during a lesson:

(Child 1), can you talk to (Child 2) AND listen to me at the SAME TIME?

Is during a math lesson a GOOD TIME or a NOT GOOD TIME to talk to (Child 2)?

## ICPS DIALOGUES

**Situation 1:** Tamika tells her teacher she doesn't like her and wants to be transferred to Mr. C's class.

Tamika:   I don't like you.

Teacher:   Oh, I'm sorry to hear that. Why do you feel that way?

Tamika:   'Cause you're mean. You yell at me.

Teacher:   When did I yell at you last?

Tamika:   Two days ago.

| Teacher: | Do you remember why I yelled? |
|---|---|
| Tamika: | No! |
| Teacher: | Think hard. What were you doing when I yelled? |
| Tamika: | I don't know. |
| Teacher: | Were you talking at a GOOD TIME or a NOT GOOD TIME? |
| Tamika: | *(Smiling)* Oh, yeah. A not good time. |
| Teacher: | How can you get me to stop yelling? |
| Tamika: | Do my work. |
| Teacher: | OK, and what else? |
| Tamika: | Stop talking so much . . . at not good times. |

*Although this teacher might have used ICPS dialoguing instead of yelling when the original incident occurred, there are times when ICPS teachers do "explode." Anger is an emotion with which children must learn to cope, although such reactions should of course not be the predominant way of handling problem situations. When Tamika brought up the incident again, the teacher helped her think it through. As the year progressed, Tamika made a concerted effort to keep from talking when it was not a good time.*

**Situation 2:** One teacher is talking to another teacher at the door when William impatiently interrupts them by saying, "I can't do this math problem."

| Teacher: | William, what am I doing right now? |
|---|---|
| William: | Talking to Ms. Roberts. |
| Teacher: | Is this a GOOD TIME or a NOT GOOD TIME to ask me to help you? |
| William: | Not a good time. |
| Teacher: | Can you think of a GOOD TIME to ask me? |
| William: | When you're finished talking. |
| Teacher: | What can you do now while you wait? |
| William: | I can't do it. I tried. |
| Teacher: | I understand that you really need help. What else can you do now? |
| William: | Work on my spelling lesson. |

*While guiding the child to think about the timing of his act, the teacher showed understanding of his immediate need. Had the teacher said, "Why don't you work on your spelling?" the child might have focused upon his need for help with the math problem instead of upon the interpersonal impact of his interrupting.*

**Situation 3:** At indoor recess, Raphael wants to play checkers, but two others are already playing.

Teacher: It looks like the game is already being used.

Raphael: But I want to play now.

Teacher: I know you do, but it looks like you'll have to wait. What can you think of to do to solve this problem?

Raphael: I can ask if I can play the winner.

Teacher: That's *one* thing you can do. If there isn't time for that, what else can you do?

Raphael: I can play at recess this afternoon.

Teacher: Good, you thought of two ideas. Can you think of something else you can do now?

Raphael: I can draw.

*The teacher avoided further frustration by helping Raphael recognize that recess time might be over before he could play the winner. Encouraging Raphael to think of his own solution helped him cope with the immediate situation. Had the teacher answered Raphael's initial request by saying, "You can't play checkers now—others are playing" and then asking, "Why don't you draw in the meantime?" Raphael would likely have whined, "I don't want to draw. I want to play checkers."*

# MEANS-ENDS THINKING

The lessons in this section are intended to encourage children to plan a sequence of steps to reach a stated interpersonal goal. Such planning, or *means-ends thinking,* requires the insight to forestall or circumvent potential obstacles, as well as the ability to command alternative routes if such obstacles appear to be insurmountable. Another component of such planning encompasses an awareness that goals are not always reached immediately (in other words, that they take time) and that certain times are more advantageous than others for action.

In brief, means-ends thinking involves the following components: goals, steps, obstacles, and statements about time.

- *Goal:* The end point, toward which effort is directed
- *Step:* An action taken to reach the goal or overcome an obstacle (in other words, a mean)
- *Obstacle:* Any event that interferes with, or could potentially interfere with, reaching the stated goal
- *Time:* Any statement referring to how long it takes to reach the stated goal or to when a particular moment to act is or is not advantageous

## PROCEDURE

The main mechanism for teaching means-ends thinking is the means-ends story, in which children identify steps, obstacles, and statements about time. As used in the lessons, the general procedure for eliciting a means-ends story is as follows:

1. State the situation and the goal. You can begin by saying, "We want to tell a very good story. Our story should have everything the person thinks about and everything the person does or says from the time that *(repeat the beginning of the story)* to the time that *(repeat the goal)*."

2. If children list unconnected alternative solutions without establishing a sequence of steps or intervening obstacles, repeat the story root and begin again, asking for a story—how one event follows another.

3. Point out the steps taken, obstacles, and statements about time.

4. If children write a story, as in Lesson 73, it should be after at least two or three means-ends stories are told orally. Otherwise, the children will not hear optimal ways such stories can evolve.

5. In all means-ends stories, children should reach the stated goal. If a child modifies the goal, repeat it as originally stated. Guide children back to the original goal and help them realize that it is important to reach the goal as stated.

6. Once the goal has been reached, stop the story. Details about what the characters in the story will do after the goal is reached are not necessary.

## SAMPLE MEANS-ENDS STORY

The following example clarifies how steps, obstacles, and statements about time interact in a story composed by children in response to Lesson 63. The statement of the problem, or story root, is as follows: "Suppose Andrew let his friend David borrow his new bike a couple of days ago, but David hasn't given it back. Andrew has to think of a *plan* to get it back."

> Andrew asks David for his bike *(Step 1)*, and David says he'll bring it back. But David doesn't bring the bike back *(Obstacle 1)*, so Andrew asks him again *(repetition of Step 1)*. David still doesn't return the bike *(repetition of Obstacle 1)*, so Andrew calls David's mother *(Step 2)*, but she is away on a trip *(Obstacle 2)*, and his father is in jail *(enumeration of Obstacle 2, adult unavailable for help)*. So Andrew tells the woman staying with David about the situation *(enumeration of Step 2, talking to an adult)*, but she doesn't want to get involved *(Obstacle 3)*. Next Andrew thinks about the situation *(Step 3)* and decides to play a trick. He calls David and tells him he needs his bike to get to the hospital quickly because his mother is sick *(Step 4)*. David doesn't believe him *(Obstacle 4)*. So Andrew thinks about waiting until David isn't home *(statement about time)* and just taking the bike, but he doesn't know how to find out when David is gone without giving his plan away *(Obstacle 5)*. Finally, Andrew tells David that if he doesn't bring the bike back they can never be friends again *(Step 5)*. So David brings the bike back *(goal)*.

# What's My Plan?

## PURPOSE

To introduce concepts relating to the development of step-by-step plans to reach stated goals

## MATERIALS

Chalkboard or easel

## TEACHER SCRIPT

We've been talking a lot about solving problems—the kind that come up between people.

We all have these kinds of problems sometimes, and it really helps to think about what to do before we act.

Up to now we've been listing DIFFERENT solutions to solve these kinds of problems.

We've also thought of consequences of those solutions.

Just as there is more than one way to solve a problem—more than one thing we can do or say, there is also more than one way to think about solving a problem.

Today we're going to talk about another way to think about solving a problem: It's called *means-ends thinking.*

To do this, we'll make up a story.

A story has a beginning and an end. It also has a middle—everything that happens between the beginning of the story and the end.

The beginning will tell about the problem a person has—the end is when the problem is solved.

First we'll think of *steps* we can take to solve the problem, to reach a *goal.*

Instead of listing DIFFERENT solutions, we'll think of a story.

In that way, we'll *plan* how to reach the goal.

The story can have in it what the person with the problem thinks about and what everyone in the story does and says.

Remember to think about how events follow one another: You don't brush your teeth before you get out of bed.

Who can think of another silly example like that?

*Let children give several examples.*

OK, the first thing we think about in our story is the steps, or means, to reach the goal.

Let's pretend my goal is to be a good race runner.

What would be some of the steps I might take?

RESPONSES: Get a coach, learn how to run and how to swing your arms, learn strategy (for example, whether to start slow or fast), enter local races and compete.

In our story, we also have to think of what might get in the way of reaching the goal—what might block it or interfere with it.

That is called an *obstacle.*

Who can think of some obstacles that could block this goal?

RESPONSES: You're not fast enough, not strong enough, don't have enough money for a coach, don't have enough time to practice.

Who can think of ways to get around these obstacles?

That's part of our plan.

RESPONSES: Exercise, weight training, practice.

Now a third thing we need to do in our story is to consider *time.* That means thinking when it is a GOOD TIME or a NOT GOOD TIME to do something and how long it will take to reach the goal.

When is a GOOD TIME to carry out the steps for the goal of becoming a good race runner?

RESPONSES: When you find a good coach, when you're healthy.

When is it a NOT GOOD TIME?

RESPONSES: In the middle of the night, when you have a lot of homework, on the day right before a big race.

How long do you think it might take to become a good race runner? (*If needed:* Would it take days? Months? Years?)

RESPONSE: Years.

*Work through a couple more examples to help children generalize these ideas. Try using the goals of getting money from a parent or going to see a friend at night, or let children state their own goals to work toward.*

## Starter Story

OK. Listen to this one.

Sharon wants her sister to do the dishes for her this weekend.

It's Sharon's turn to do them this weekend, but she got an invitation to an overnight party at her friend's house.

Now, Sharon can't just say, "I hope my sister will do the dishes" and have her magically do them.

We need a story of everything that happens from the time Sharon thinks about this to the time her sister says she'll do the dishes this weekend.

The end of the story is the *goal*.

Sharon's goal is _____. (*If needed:* To get her sister to do the dishes.)

OK. Now what *steps* should Sharon take?

Maybe she thinks to herself, "What can I do so my sister will do the dishes for me?"

That's Step 1, thinking about what to do.

"I'll tell her about all the things I've done for her." That's Step 2.

"Then I'll show her the invitation to the party (Step 3), and ask her if she'll do the dishes for me (Step 4)."

The sister says yes, and that's the goal.

*Write the steps as given in a column on the left side of the chalkboard, as shown in the example at the end of this lesson.*

Do you think the problem can always be solved that easily?

Remember, when something blocks a plan, or gets in the way of the goal, that is called an *obstacle*.

Are there any obstacles? (*If needed:* Is there anything Sharon's sister might say or do that would stop the plan?)

RESPONSE: Her sister might get mad 'cause she doesn't think Sharon does enough favors for her.

If Sharon's sister gets mad, that's an obstacle because it blocks Sharon's goal.

*Write obstacles as they are given in a second column, as shown in the example.*

Now there's a third thing to think about. Who remembers?

Yes, time.

If Sharon is going to ask her sister or talk to her, it is a NOT GOOD TIME _____.

RESPONSE: When her sister is in a bad mood.

*Write statements about time in a third column, as shown in the example.*

Remember, sometimes you can wait too long. You have to plan ahead.

If Sharon asks her sister right after dinner, at the last minute, is that a GOOD TIME or a NOT GOOD TIME?

Why?

When is a GOOD TIME?

RESPONSE: After Sharon has done something for her.

OK, now let's look at these steps carefully.
*(Refer to the board—see example on page 347.)*

If Sharon's sister thinks she doesn't do enough favors for her, she'll have to change her plan right here. *(Indicate Step 2 and draw an arrow from Step 2 to Obstacle 1.)*

Maybe that's when Sharon shows her sister the party invitation and asks her, but her sister says no. *(Draw an arrow from Step 3 to Obstacle 2.)*

Let's continue the story. Look at the obstacles and the ideas about time.

You can make up new steps to go around the obstacles.

Be sure you end the story with Sharon's sister doing the dishes for her this weekend, even though it's Sharon turn to do them.

*Use the model of the Continuation Game illustrated in Lesson 17 to have children complete the story: One person makes up a sentence or two in the story and then says, "Continuation." Another then takes up where the first person left off, and so forth. Add responses to the appropriate columns in the chart.*

*If a child ends the story too soon, ask for an obstacle that might get in the way of the plan. Write any new steps, obstacles, or statements about time under their appropriate headings.*

*If a child lists unconnected solutions instead of continuing the story in a step-wise fashion, say, "Remember, now we're telling a really good story—everything that happens from the beginning to the end. We need steps, obstacles, and thoughts about time."*

*When the story is complete, count the number of steps, obstacles, and statements about time and list these totals on the board.*

| Steps | Obstacles | Time |
|---|---|---|
| 1. Thinks about what to do. | 1. Sister gets mad because she thinks Sharon does not do enough favors for her. | 1. When her sister is in a bad mood. *(Not good)* |
| 2. Tells sister all the things she's done for her. | 2. Sister says no. | 2. At the last minute, right before Sharon wants her sister to do them. *(Not good)* |
| 3. Shows her the party invitation. | 3. Sister says yes but then gets sick. | 3. Right after Sharon has done something for her. *(Good)* |
| 4. Asks her to do the dishes. | | |

# A Problem-Solving Plan, Part I

## PURPOSE

To strengthen children's understanding of concepts relating to the development of step-by-step plans to reach stated goals

## MATERIALS

Chalkboard or easel

## TEACHER SCRIPT

Today we're going to think again about *steps, obstacles,* and *time* as they relate to reaching a *goal.*

Think of this as a television show: Suppose Andrew let his friend David borrow his new bike a couple of days ago, but David hasn't given it back.

Andrew has to think of a *plan* to get it back.

Uh-oh. Your television set just went off. I wonder what's happening?

Well, the television set just came back on.

It's the end of the show, and there's Andrew with his bike back. What happened while the television set was off?

Let's think of everything that might have happened from the time Andrew first let David borrow his bike to the time Andrew got his bike back.

Let's make up a real good story.

*Use the model of the Continuation Game described in Lesson 17. Write the story on the chalkboard as it unfolds. Guiding questions, if necessary, can be as follows:*

What's the first thing Andrew thinks about? Step 1?

What's Step 2? What might he do next?

Is there anything that could block that step? An obstacle?

What can he do to get around that obstacle?

When is a GOOD TIME to take that step?

What about a NOT GOOD TIME?

How long might it take for Andrew to reach this goal?

What's the very next thing that happens in this story?

*Continue in this manner, modifying questions to fit the story until the goal is reached. After the goal is reached:*

How did Andrew feel before he solved his problem?

How did Andrew feel after he solved his problem?

*Have the class identify steps, obstacles, and statements about time. List them as for Lesson 62, drawing arrows from the steps to the obstacles connected to them. Alternatively, circle the various components on the board in different colored chalk. Count the number of steps, obstacles, and statements about time and write these totals on the board.*

# Mystery Sequence

## PURPOSE

To encourage sequential thinking, essential for the development of means-ends plans

## MATERIALS

Illustrations 30–32

Scissors

Paper

Tape or paste

## TEACHER SCRIPT

*Give each child a copy of Illustrations 30–32, a pair of scissors, paper, and tape or paste.*

Today's game is called Mystery Sequence.

You have in front of you seven pictures, but they are not in the right order.

They are not what would happen first, second, third, and so on.

Think about a story these pictures could tell and number them in the order you want them.

There is more than one way you can arrange these pictures to make a logical story: There is no right way or wrong way.

Next, cut out the pictures and tape or paste to blank sheets in story order. (*Or:* Arrange them in order on your desk.)

A balloon with wavy lines is for what the person is thinking.

A balloon with smooth lines is for what the person is saying.

Write your story inside the balloons.

Include what the person is thinking and what the person is saying.

*Let children read their stories as time and interest permit. Display the finished stories on a bulletin board, if desired.*

Number _____

Number _____

ILLUSTRATION 30   Lesson 64

Number _____

Number _____

ILLUSTRATION 31   Lesson 64

Number _____

Number _____

Number _____

ILLUSTRATION 32   Lesson 64

# Sequencing

## READING AND STORY COMPREHENSION

*Read a story, then ask:*

What might have happened before the story started?

What happened before _____? *(Describe an event from the story.)*

What happened after _____? *(Describe the same event.)*

What happened next?

What followed that?

*(Choose an event in the middle of the story.)* Did _____ happen before OR after _____? *(Describe another event.)*

What might happen 5 years after the story ends?

What else?

## MATH

Here are some sets of numbers. What comes next?

4, 6, 8, _____.

3, 6, 9, _____.

$2 \times 2, 3 \times 3, 4 \times 4,$ _____.

$\frac{4}{2}, \frac{9}{3}, \frac{16}{4},$ _____.

*Use concepts the class is learning. If a child answers incorrectly, ask how he or she came to that answer. Let the child describe his or her thinking process.*

## SCIENCE

How a plant grows . . .

Step 1: Plant the seed.

Step 2: Water the area where the seed is planted.

*Let the class complete the sequence. Encourage them to draw pictures of the events and number the order of their occurrence.*

## SOCIAL STUDIES

How the Declaration of Independence was signed . . .

What happened first? *(The King of England unfairly taxed the colonists.)*

Then? *(The colonists met to decide on independence.)*

Then? *(The First Continental Congress met.)*

Then? *(The Second Continental Congress drafted and adopted the Declaration of Independence.)*

Then? *(The Revolutionary War started.)*

Then? *(The colonists won the war.)*

Then? *(The 13 colonies were independent.)*

# Will the Person Be Angry?

## PURPOSE

To review the process of generating multiple solutions
(in contrast to sequential, means-ends thinking)

## MATERIALS

Chalkboard or easel

Activity Sheets 18 and 19

## TEACHER SCRIPT

*Give each child a copy of Activity Sheets 18 and 19. Follow this procedure for each sheet. Directions are written for Activity Sheet 18; modify as necessary for Activity Sheet 19.*

1. Read the problem aloud.

2. Say, "Some things the kid could do or say might make the kid's mother feel ANGRY. For this, we're going to think about solutions again, lots of DIFFERENT solutions, but not a story."

3. Instruct children to write lots of different solutions to the problem of spilling sugar on the floor, solutions that might make the kid's mother feel angry.

4. Next instruct children to write lots of different solutions that might not make the kid's mother feel angry.

5. Let the class read their solutions out loud and vote on which one to discuss for consequences. Consequences should include those other than feelings (in other words, what the mother might do or say if the child did or said a particular thing).

6. Choose two children to role-play the problem. Prompt the role-players to first think of and present several solutions identified as ones that would likely make the mother angry, then to end with a solution that would likely not make her angry. The following example was created by two fourth graders:

    Child:   I could let you clean up the mess.

    Mother:   I'm still angry.

    Child:   I could clean it up later.

    Mother:   I'm still angry.

Child:   Let's just leave it the way it is.

Mother:   I'm still angry.

Child:   I'll clean it up right now.

Mother:   OK.

7. Once the child playing the role of the mother says OK to a particular solution, ask that child why the solution does not make her feel angry.

**Problem:** This kid spilled sugar all over the kitchen floor.

Solutions that will probably make the mother feel angry:

Solutions that will probably NOT make the mother feel angry:

**Problem:** One kid wants to borrow the other's roller skates, but the kid on the skates pays no attention.

Solutions that will probably make the kid on skates feel angry:

Solutions that will probably NOT make the kid on skates feel angry:

# How Could I Avoid This Problem?

## PURPOSE

To combine previous lesson content in a new way, in order to help children appreciate how actions affect others

## MATERIALS

Mini-Play 13

## TEACHER SCRIPT

---

**NOTE**

Make a copy of Mini-Play 13 for each actor, then circle each actor's part.

---

*Choose two children to perform Mini-Play 13, then ask the following questions:*

What didn't Arthur remember about what Kenneth likes?

What did Kenneth think Arthur meant when he said he spent all of something?

Why did Kenneth think that? (*If needed:* What did Kenneth do when Arthur was talking? Listen or interrupt?)

How did Arthur feel when he found out he didn't remember what Kenneth likes?

How did Kenneth feel when he called Arthur stupid for the wrong reason?

What is the problem between these two kids?

How could this problem have been avoided? You know, what could have kept the problem from happening in the first place?

Does anyone see a DIFFERENT problem?

How could *that* problem have been avoided?

Can you think of a problem you could have avoided if you had remembered something about someone?

Had listened and not interrupted?

Any other way?

## WHAT DID I SPEND?

Arthur:    Kenneth, I remembered that you once told me you like
to play baseball, so I spent all . . .

Kenneth:    Oh, you shouldn't have bought me a baseball bat.
You didn't remember right. I told you I like *basketball.*

Arthur:    Oh, I feel so embarrassed. And I spent all . . .

Kenneth:    You spent all—your money. You're stupid!

Arthur:    I didn't spend all my money. I didn't buy you
a baseball bat. I spent all morning going to buy
tickets so I could take you to a baseball game.

Kenneth:    Oh, now *I'm* embarrassed.

# Means-Ends Review

## PURPOSE

To break down means-ends thinking into its individual components, in order to help those children still having difficulty with this thought process

## MATERIALS

None

## TEACHER SCRIPT

Today I'm going to tell you some *goals,* and you tell me some *steps,* some *obstacles,* and some GOOD TIMES and NOT GOOD TIMES to take those steps.

You've already done this in the stories you've told, but now we're going to talk about them one at a time.

I'll start with some real easy ones.

Remember, we need steps, obstacles, and times when we try to plan ways to reach a goal.

That's DIFFERENT from listing DIFFERENT solutions because here the whole plan leads to the goal.

When we think of solutions, we think of lots of DIFFERENT ideas.

For means-ends thinking, we think about _____.
(*If needed:* How one thing follows another, a sequence of events.)

*Call on children who did not participate actively in Lessons 62 and 63 or who seem to be having difficulty with means-ends thinking.*

## Example 1

OK. Here's the first one. I'll start it.

Suppose your goal is to play at the playground. You are now at home.

Step 1 is _____. (*For example:* To think about how to do it, to get on the bus.)

*If "playing ball" or another like response is given, say, "Wait, something's missing. First you have to get to the playground. How do you get there?"*

Can you think of an obstacle that might get in the way of your getting to the playground? (*For example:* A friend stops you and talks, someone knocks you down.)

When is a GOOD TIME to take Step 1?

What about a NOT GOOD TIME?

## Example 2

Your goal is to call a friend on the phone.

You can't just pick up the phone and say hello.

What do you have to do first? What is Step 1?
(*For example:* Dial, push the buttons.)

What obstacles might get in the way of your reaching this goal? (*For example:* The line is busy, your friend isn't home, your friend's mother says he's eating dinner.)

When is a GOOD TIME to take Step 1?

When is a NOT GOOD TIME?

## Example 3

Your goal is to get milk for your breakfast. There is no milk in your house.

What is Step 1?

Are there any obstacles to Step 1?

When is a GOOD TIME to take the first step?

And a NOT GOOD TIME?

Let's take this a little further. If (*repeat obstacle*) happens, what's the next thing that happens in the story, Step 2?

*Continue asking for obstacles and statements about time until the goal is reached.*

## Example 4

OK, now I'm going to make this a little harder.

The goal is for a girl to use her brother's new record player.

What is Step 1?

Are there any obstacles to Step 1?

When is a GOOD TIME to take Step 1?

And a NOT GOOD TIME?

Let's take this a little further. If (*repeat obstacle*) happens, what is the next thing that happens in the story, Step 2?

*Continue asking for obstacles and statements about time until the goal is reached.*

*If desired, let children make up a goal that involves at least one other person, then repeat the previous line of questioning. Continue for as long as children take to reach the goal (no fewer than three steps).*

---

**HINT**

When real problems come up, dialogue and/or encourage those involved to role-play. Children who role-play can now be given the choice of acting out solutions or devising means-ends plans. You may want to try pairing a child having difficulty solving an actual problem with a more competent problem solver.

---

# Means-Ends Dialoguing

*When means-ends thinking would help solve a problem, you may wish to try a means-ends dialogue, as the following example illustrates.*

> **Situation:** Jody tells the teacher she lost her best friend because they had an argument.

> Teacher: What happened? What caused your friend to get mad?

> Jody: She told me a secret, and I told my friend, and she found out.

> Teacher: Jody, what is your goal? What do you want the ending to be?

> Jody: I want my friend back. I want us to make up.

> Teacher: OK, what's the first thing you can do or say to end up having your friend back? The first step?

> Jody: I can say I'm sorry. I'll never do that again.

> Teacher: How will you do that?

> Jody: I'll call her on the phone.

> Teacher: Is there anything that could block that step—an obstacle?

> Jody: Her mother will answer and say she's not home.

> Teacher: How will you get around that obstacle?

> Jody: I'll wait till recess and find her on the playground.

> Teacher: If she has lots of children around her, would that be a GOOD TIME or a NOT GOOD TIME to talk to her about this?

> Jody: A not good time.

> Teacher: When is a GOOD TIME?

> Jody: Maybe when she's by herself.

> Teacher: OK, then what might happen?

> Jody: She'll probably still be mad.

> Teacher: That's another obstacle to your goal. What will your next step be?

> Jody: I'll have a party in her honor. But I'll wait a few weeks so maybe she'll miss me.

Teacher: How will you get her to come?
What steps will you take?

Jody: I'll invite her best friends and tell them
to tell her I have a special present for her,
and I'll write her an extra pretty invitation.
Now she'll know how much I care.

Teacher: And then?

Jody: She'll come, and I'll tell her I want to be her friend,
and she'll say, "Let's make up."

*This kind of dialoguing helps children think through a plan, a sequenced series of steps. Recognizing potential obstacles helps them appreciate that problem solving is not always smooth sailing. Thinking about a good versus not a good time helps children think in a less impulsive way.*

# Means-Ends Thinking

*Let the class create and write a story about one of the following:*

- A police officer, fire fighter, mayor, or person in another job or profession
- An historical event (for example, Martin Luther King's civil rights plan, Columbus's arrival in America, space exploration)
- A social problem (for example, water/air/noise pollution, smoking, alcohol/drug abuse, child abuse)

*Tell the class the story should include:*

- The goal
- Steps to reach the goal (a plan)
- Obstacles (either physical or social) that could get in the way of reaching the goal
- Ways to get around the obstacles (more steps in the plan)
- Statements about time (a GOOD TIME or a NOT GOOD TIME, how long it will take to reach the goal)

*Have the class circle steps, obstacles, and statements about time and chart them, as illustrated in Lesson 62.*

# Full Use of ICPS Concepts

## READING AND STORY COMPREHENSION

*Read any story that contains some kind of problem, whether interpersonal or not. Choose from the following questions to fit the particular story being discussed.*

### Problem Identification, Feelings, Solutions/Consequences

What happened? What's the problem?

What is relevant information in the story to help us identify the problem?

What is NOT relevant information?

Why might (Character 1) have done that?

Any other reason?

How did (Character 2) feel when (Character 1) did that? How can you tell?

What happened next when (he/she) did that? What did (Character 2) do or say next?

How did (Character 1) feel when (Character 2) did or said that?

What did (Character 1) do or say to solve the problem?

What else could (Character 1) have said or done to solve the problem?

Is that a good idea? Why or why NOT?

### Means-Ends Thinking

What was the goal _____ had? *(Name a character from the story.)*

What did (he/she) do first? And then?

Did (he/she) pick a GOOD TIME or a NOT GOOD TIME to do that?

What happened after (he/she) did that?

Did anything get in the way of (his/her) reaching the goal? Were there any obstacles?

Then what did (he/she) do? What was (his/her) next step?

How long it did take (him/her) to reach the goal?

## SOCIAL STUDIES

*Let the class fill in as much as they can using the components of means-ends thinking: steps, obstacles, and statements about time.*

>**Example 1:** A community problem, such as one encountered by the recreation department, police department, department of sanitation, or city council
>
>What's the problem?
>
>How might _____ feel about that?
>
>What can _____ do to solve the problem?
>
>What might get in the way (an obstacle)?
>
>Then what could _____ do?
>
>How long might that take?

>**Example 2:** An historical event, such as the Native Americans' sale of their land to the English settlers
>
>What happened? What was the problem?
>
>How did the Native Americans feel when that happened?
>
>What could they have done so that would NOT have happened?
>
>What might have gotten in the way if they tried that (an obstacle)?
>
>Then what could they have done?
>
>What would be a GOOD TIME to do that?

*Other examples of historical events might include George Washington's plan for the colonies' independence from the British, Abraham Lincoln's plan to free the slaves, Martin Luther King's plan for civil rights, or Susan B. Anthony's plan for women's right to vote. Tell a story and include steps, obstacles, and statements about time (for example, a good time to fight, how long the Revolutionary War took). Encourage children to think of their own examples.*

## SCIENCE

>**Example 1:** A plant or fish dying before it should have
>
>What happened? What's the matter?
>
>Why do you think that happened?
>
>Why else?
>
>How would you feel if that happened to you?
>
>What could you do so that wouldn't happen?
>
>And then what?

**Example 2:** Too much pollution in the air

What kind of pollution is in the air?

Why do you think that is true?

What can we do about that?

What might block the goal (an obstacle)?

What can we do to get around that obstacle?

Then what would we do?

# A Problem-Solving Plan, Part II

## PURPOSE

To strengthen children's understanding of concepts relating to the development of step-by-step plans to reach stated goals

## MATERIALS

Chalkboard or easel

## TEACHER SCRIPT

Today I'm going to tell you a story about a boy with a problem.

I'm going to tell you the beginning, the middle, and the end.

Listen carefully: You tell me what's missing in the middle of this story.

There is going to be a school play 6 months from now, and Devin wants the part of the television newscaster.

Another boy, Julius, also wants the part. That's the beginning.

The middle of the story is that Devin wishes he could have the part.

The story ends with Devin's having the part and Julius's not being mad.

What's missing in the middle of this story? (*If needed:* We need to fill in how Devin got the part without making Julius mad.)

Let's start from the beginning.

*Use the model of the Continuation Game described in Lesson 17. Write the story on the chalkboard and count steps, obstacles, and statements about time. If necessary, ask the following questions:*

What's the first thing Devin thinks about when he wants the part of the television newscaster?

Then what happens?

Are there any obstacles that could get in the way?

Does Devin get the part after he takes the first step, or does his plan need more steps?

How do the people in this story feel about what happens?

*(Repeat a given step.)* When is a GOOD TIME to take this step?

When is a NOT GOOD TIME?

Remember to end the story so Devin gets the part and so Julius isn't mad.

How did Devin feel before he got the part?

How did Devin feel after he solved this problem?

# Feeling Cartoons, Part III

## PURPOSE

To provide further illustration of how DIFFERENT people can feel DIFFERENT ways

## MATERIALS

Activity Sheets 20 and 21

## TEACHER SCRIPT

*Give each child a copy of Activity Sheets 20 and 21. Remind children of the procedures given in Lessons 18 and 43 for completing these sheets.*

## OPTIONS

1. Have children write down different things each person pictured might be thinking, avoiding enumerations.

2. More difficult: Have children choose one character and write how he or she feels about something. Have them use the feeling words associated with each of the other characters to describe why all the characters feel the way they do about the same event. (This may be easiest to do orally.)

### Example 1

The boy is EMBARRASSED because he fell and his knee is bleeding.

The other boy feels SYMPATHETIC towards him.

The teacher is HAPPY because the boy didn't hurt himself badly.

His father is PROUD because the boy washed his knee and put a bandage on by himself.

### Example 2

The teacher is HAPPY because a girl in her class did all her homework.

The boy is EMBARRASSED because he didn't do his.

The other boy feels SYMPATHETIC towards him and tries to help him.

The other boy's father is PROUD of that boy for helping.

**DIFFERENT people can feel DIFFERENT ways**

EMBARRASSED

PROUD

# DIFFERENT people can feel DIFFERENT ways

**SYMPATHETIC**

**HAPPY**

# Guess the Problem, Part I

## PURPOSE

To develop sensitivity to cues as to what a problem is and to encourage awareness that it is not always possible to tell what a problem is without further information

## MATERIALS

Any hand puppet (optional)

## TEACHER SCRIPT

---

**NOTE**

This lesson may be conducted over 2 days, if desired. Write each of the problem situations listed at the end of this lesson (or problem situations of your own devising) on slips of paper before the lesson begins.

---

Today we're going to play a guessing game.

We're going to guess what the problem is.

To play this game, we're going to *pantomime*, or *mime*.

Remember before when we did this with feeling words.

We used our faces or moved our bodies but did NOT use any words.

Now I'll show you how I can mime a problem between people.

*Hold the puppet in one hand. Pretend to eat something with your other hand— show in your expression that you really like it. Pull the puppet toward you and move the puppet's mouth to show that the puppet wants some of the food. Shake your head no. (If a puppet is not available, you can pretend to pour liquid from a pitcher into a glass and drink, then grimace to show you don't like the taste.)*

Can you guess what's happening?

What did I do that made you think that?

What else did I do?

*Divide the class into groups of four to six children each, then give each group the slip of paper with their problem situation. If the group desires, they can make up their own problem situation.*

OK. We're going to divide up into groups.

I have a problem, written on a piece of paper, that came up between kids.

First, I'll give one to Group 1.

You go out in the hall for a few minutes and decide how you're going to mime it.

It's good if you can practice it once.

When you come back, the class will try to guess what the problem is.

Remember, only facial expressions and body movements—no words.

*After the group mimes their problem, let one child guess what it is.*

(*To the child who guesses*) How do you think the person(s) felt?

What did the person(s) do that made you think that?

What did the person(s) do that made you guess the problem you did?

(*To the actors*) Was that the problem you were miming?

*If the correct problem is not guessed, repeat the process with a few more children. If the problem is still not guessed, say, "Sometimes we need more information before we know what problem someone is having," then have the actors add words to the presentation:*

Now you can use words.

But try not to give away the whole problem.

Try to give just one clue at a time.

*After each new clue is given, ask the group if they can guess the problem. Point out any false assumptions and stress that things are not always what they seem to be. Ask, "What facts told you what the real problem is?"*

*If time and interest permit, let the group role-play solutions and consequences. If necessary, encourage the child offering a solution to try another if the first one offered does not work. Repeat this process with remaining groups.*

390

## Problem Situations

1. A group is playing jump rope. One boy runs into the rope and ruins the game.

2. A group is standing in line to get a drink of water. One boy tries to get a drink out of turn, pushing away another kid at the fountain.

3. A group is playing ball. While chasing the ball, one girl pushes into another accidentally, but the others think it is on purpose.

4. A group is playing hopscotch, and another child is watching. She wants to get into the game, but the other kids won't let her.

5. A group is playing musical instruments. One child doesn't have an instrument and wants a turn to try one. Each child in the group says no.

*If these are too obvious, try the following:*

6. A group is at a birthday party. One boy spills milk on another's clothes. The other boy thinks the first boy did it on purpose.

7. A group is cleaning up, putting things away. One girl won't help. The group tries to get her to, but she still won't.

# Guess the Problem, Part II

## PURPOSE

To enhance skills of logical deduction and to help children further classify types of problems

## MATERIALS

Chalkboard or easel

## TEACHER SCRIPT

*First play the game 20 Questions as it is usually played, using the categories animal, vegetable, or mineral so children can get the idea of logical deduction. Begin with easy objects to deduce—for example, a dog or cat. After the game is played:*

Today we're going to guess a people problem in the same way we just played 20 Questions.

Someone will make up a people problem like the ones we've been talking about in ICPS, and the rest of you will try to figure it out by asking questions that can be answered yes or no.

The problem can be between two kids, a teacher and a whole class, a teacher and one kid, a mother and her daughter or son, and so forth.

I'll show you what I mean: Let's say I'm thinking of the problem that one boy lets another play with his ball, but the second boy won't give it back.

First, I find out how many people are involved. Who knows?

RESPONSE: Two.

Second, I find out who the problem is between. Who can tell us this?

RESPONSE: Two kids.

Third, I find out what feelings are involved. Who can guess this?

RESPONSE: Anger, disappointment.

Fourth, I find out who has the feelings. Who would have these feelings?

RESPONSE: One kid feels that way about the other.

Now I ask questions to figure out the problem.

I can't just go after it "shot-in-the-dark."

I have to ask questions that will help me figure the problem out. When we played 20 Questions before, you didn't just guess the answer right off the bat.

First you had to know something about what you were guessing—that it was an animal, that it had four legs, and so on.

In this game, we have to find out something about the problem before we guess it.

In the problem about the boy who won't give the ball back, I *can* ask: Is the kid mad at the other for not keeping his promise to do something?

I *can't* ask: Is the kid mad at the other boy because the other boy hit him? That's a shot-in-the-dark guess.

I *can* ask: Is he mad because the other boy wasn't fair about something?

Since the answer to that is yes, now I can guess what he wasn't fair about (for example, sharing something, returning something, wanting something when it wasn't his turn).

It isn't necessary to guess the specific object that wasn't returned (in this case, a ball), but you can discuss the general nature of the problem (in this case, having someone not return something borrowed).

You can discuss possible consequences of not returning a borrowed object, how the lender might feel, and so on.

*Pick a leader to make up an interpersonal problem and have him or her whisper it in your ear. Then say to the group:*

OK, now you can ask 20 questions that can be answered yes or no to discover the secret.

I'm going to put four starter clues on the board. They don't count in the number of questions asked.

*The starter clues concern how many people are involved, who is involved, the feelings associated with the problem, and who has those feelings.*

*(After the four clues are established)* OK, remember to ask questions to figure this out.

Don't guess the problem in a shot-in-the-dark way.

## OPTION

Divide the group into two teams and give each team a separate problem to figure out. First Team A plays, then Team B. The team that figures out the problem in the fewest number of questions wins.

# A Problem-Solving Plan, Part III

## PURPOSE

To strengthen children's understanding of concepts relating to the development of step-by-step plans to reach stated goals

## MATERIALS

None

## TEACHER SCRIPT

Today we're going to think about a *plan* again.

I'm going to tell you the beginning and the end of a story about a problem between people—this time about three sisters.

You make up the middle of the story.

We'll play this game the way we did before.

Here's the problem: Three sisters, ages 11, 9, and 7, are at home, and their parents are going out for the evening.

Their next door neighbor, age 23, offers to take them out, but each of the sisters wants to do something DIFFERENT.

The 11-year-old wants to go roller skating, the 9-year-old wants to go bowling, and the 7-year-old wants to go to a movie.

The neighbor says to the 11-year-old, "I will do whatever you decide, but I want you to be in charge of solving this problem."

The story ends with the problem solved and everybody HAPPY.

One catch—no one goes off alone.

Make up a really good story from the time the neighbor discovers that everyone wants to do something DIFFERENT to the time the problem is solved and everybody is HAPPY.

Tell us everything that was said or done in this story.

*Use the model of the Continuation Game described in Lesson 17. Write the story on the chalkboard as it unfolds. If necessary, ask the following guiding questions:*

OK, the first thing that happens in the story is _____.

How does each person in the story feel in the beginning?

What is the first thing that is said or done?

What is the first step the 11-year-old takes?

Does anything happen (or does anyone say anything) that makes it hard for the 11-year-old to solve this problem? Any obstacles?

What is the next thing that is said or done?

What are GOOD TIMES for the 11-year-old to take her steps?

*When the story is completed, point out and count the steps, obstacles, and statements about time.*

# A Problem-Solving Plan, Part IV

## PURPOSE

To strengthen children's understanding of concepts relating to the development of step-by-step plans to reach stated goals

## MATERIALS

Activity Sheet 22

## TEACHER SCRIPT

*Give each child a copy of Activity Sheet 22.*

I'm going to give you the beginning and the end of a story about a boy who had a problem.

You fill in the middle, but this time, I want you to write it down.

Here's the situation: Ron used to watch the other kids play, but he was too shy and scared to join in.

But now he's a good problem solver, and he's not shy and scared anymore.

One day he saw some kids playing tag, and he said to himself, "I'm going to figure out a plan to get into that game."

The story ends with Ron's being in the game.

Write a story about what happens between the time Ron decides to think of a plan to get into the game of tag and the end of the story, when he is in the game.

*Encourage children to include steps, obstacles, and statements about time in their stories.*

## OPTIONS

1. Let a child read his or her story aloud. If necessary, guide by asking:

   - What was Ron's first step?
   - Then what happened? *(If anything is missing, point it out, backtrack, and help the child fill in the gap.)*
   - Were there any obstacles?
   - Did Ron pick a GOOD TIME or a NOT GOOD TIME to take the step?

   Point out and count the steps, obstacles, and statements about time initially given, then note any added in presentation and review of the story.

2. Let the children circle all the steps, obstacles, and statements about time in their own stories, identifying each with the letters *S*, *O*, and *T*. If you wish, you can collect the stories and check these.

3. For maximum participation, do Option 2 in addition to Option 1.

**Goal** _____

_____

**My story** _____

_____

_____

_____

_____

_____

_____

_____

_____

_____

_____

_____

_____

_____

_____

_____

_____

_____

_____

**Write down the number of:**

Steps _____ Obstacles _____ Good times _____ Not good times _____

# A Problem-Solving Plan, Part V

## PURPOSE

To strengthen children's understanding of concepts relating to the development of step-by-step plans to reach stated goals

## MATERIALS

Chalkboard or easel

## TEACHER SCRIPT

Today we're going to think again of a plan to solve a problem.

What are the three things we have to think about when we think of a plan? (*If needed:* Steps, _____, and _____.)

*Choose from among the following story roots, or let children devise their own.*

1. Terrance told some kids that he is going to fight Benji after school today. One of the kids, Zachery, told Benji about it. Benji is scared and doesn't want Terrance to fight him. The story ends up so they don't fight and so the kids don't tease Benji for being scared.

2. Anthony saw two kids fighting, and he decided he would try to help them stop. The story ends with Anthony's helping the kids solve their problem and everybody being HAPPY.

3. Patty wants to be on the baseball team, but the kids say no. The story ends with Patty on the team and everyone being HAPPY.

4. Carol was supposed to meet Diane at the movies at 2:00. Carol was on time and waited and waited for Diane. Diane never showed up. Carol was very mad at Diane. The story ends up with Carol's not being mad at Diane.

**OPTIONS**

1. Play the Continuation Game (described in Lesson 17): Ask questions like those in Lesson 62 to draw out steps, obstacles, and statements about time.

2. Let one child tell a story the whole way through. Ask the class to comment on anything that might be missing.

3. Let the whole class write a story, following the procedure for Lesson 73. Have each child circle his or her own steps, obstacles, and statements about time.

# A Dilemma

## PURPOSE

To combine all ICPS skills learned—consideration of one's own and others' feelings, solutions, consequences, and means-ends thinking

## MATERIALS

Mini-Play 14

## TEACHER SCRIPT

Today we're going to have another mini-play.

I need a girl to play the mother and a boy to play her son.

This is a different kind of problem.

It's called a *dilemma*.

This boy has to choose one of two things to do, and whichever one he chooses, someone is going to feel bad.

*Choose two actors to read Mini-Play 14. Then let the child playing Paul give solutions (or describe a plan). Let the child playing the mother respond to the solutions (or plan). When the performance is complete, ask the following questions:*

How did Paul get himself into this mess in the first place?

What does he think about before deciding what to do?

How might Alan feel if Paul doesn't go to the game?

How might Paul's sister feel if Paul doesn't go to the party?

How might Paul's mother feel about that?

How does Paul feel about all this?

*If solutions were given, choose one or let the class vote on one:*

What might the people in this story do or say if _____?
*(Repeat the solution chosen.)*

Which solutions will help make both Alan and Paul's
sister feel HAPPY?

Can anyone think of a DIFFERENT solution that will help
Alan and Paul's sister feel HAPPY?

*If a means-ends plan is given, and if time and interest permit:*

Can anyone think of a DIFFERENT plan to solve this problem?

## A DILEMMA

Paul:   Mom, Alan's mother has an extra ticket to the baseball game today, and Alan asked me to go. I'm so excited.

Mother:   Uh-oh, did you say yes?

Paul:   Yep! I really want to go.

Mother:   Don't you remember today's your sister's birthday? We're going to give her a party. Don't you care about that?

Paul:   Yeah. Now what do I do?

Mother:   What do you think you can do? Can you think of something?

# A Problem-Solving Plan, Part VI

## PURPOSE

To strengthen children's understanding of concepts relating to the development of step-by-step plans to reach stated goals

## MATERIALS

None

## TEACHER SCRIPT

Today we have another dilemma.

This time, we're going to think of a *plan* to solve it.

Who remembers what we have to think about when we think of a plan? (*If needed:* Steps, _____, and _____.)

Here's the problem: Tracy says to Charise, "Why don't you want Francine to come to my birthday party?"

"Because I don't like her, and she'll ruin the party," answers Charise.

"But, Charise, she's my best friend. I feel worried and sad not to invite her."

But Charise says, "If you invite Francine, I won't come."

Tracy wants both Charise and Francine to come to her party.

The story ends up with both of them coming and everyone feeling HAPPY about it.

## OPTIONS

1. Play the Continuation Game (described in Lesson 17): Ask questions like those in Lesson 62 to draw out steps, obstacles, and statements about time.

2. Let one child tell a story the whole way through. Ask the class to comment on anything that might be missing.

3. Let the whole class write a story, following the procedure for Lesson 73. Have each child circle his or her own steps, obstacles, and statements about time.

# Looking Forward

## PURPOSE

To anticipate potential problems children may encounter in the next school year, in order to help reduce the stress of this transition

## MATERIALS

None

## TEACHER SCRIPT

Today we're going to talk about some real problems.

First, someone tell us about a problem you had with someone at home, at school, or anywhere.

Tell us how you would have solved that problem before.

How did you solve it, or could you have solved it, now that you've had ICPS?

Which way do you think is better?

Why?

*Repeat with a few more children. If children talk only of problems relating to fighting, ask for a problem that is different from fighting.*

OK. Now we're going to talk about something DIFFERENT.

Next fall you'll be going on to _____. *(Name the next grade.)*

Tell us what about going on to _____ makes you feel excited. *(Let children respond.)*

Now think for a minute about some problems you might have in _____.

What makes you feel AFRAID or WORRIED?

OK, let's talk about the problem.

Let's start with DIFFERENT solutions.

*Elicit solutions and consequences as before. If the problem is conducive to construction of a means-ends plan, ask someone to tell a story, including steps, obstacles, and statements about time. You may wish to let children role-play a problem they foresee. Repeat with as many different problems as time and interest permit.*

# APPENDIX A

# Guidelines for Continued ICPS Teaching

Teaching does not stop once the formal ICPS lessons have been completed. If children are to associate how they think with what they do, you must continue to make frequent use of the ICPS dialoguing approach when interacting with children informally in the classroom. This association may be critical to how problem-solving thinking can guide behavior. It is also important to apply ICPS principles consistently whenever opportunities arise.

When the last lesson is completed, ask the class the following questions:

1. Why do you think we did ICPS?

2. Do you like it when you think for yourselves?

3. What did you learn to think about when these kinds of problems come up? Anything else? *(Try to elicit feelings, solutions, consequences, plans—steps, obstacles, times—listening, and so on.)*

4. Who solved a problem recently? Did you do something different than you did (would have done) before? Which way do you think is better? Why?

The following general suggestions can help you keep ICPS alive in your classroom after the lessons are over:

1. Apply ICPS teaching to the stories you read or reread in class. At any point, ask children if they remember what happens next or, for a new story, to guess what might happen next. Encourage children to draw the problem, characters' feelings, and how the problem was solved. Discuss, either in small groups or as a class, then let children role-play part of the story.

2. Let children choose from available puppets and create problems to role-play. They can also role-play actual problems. As "puppets" try to solve the problem, tell them to call on children in class for a new solution.

3. When an actual problem comes up, encourage the children involved to draw what happened, name solutions, and present the problem to the class for more solutions.

4. Ask children to role-play real or fictitious problems, solutions, and consequences. Then the role-players can call on others to have a turn.

411

Quiz yourself periodically on how ICPS is working for you as a teacher. Ask yourself whether you can think of a time when:

1. You made a child in your class feel:
   a. happy
   b. angry
   c. sad
   d. afraid
   e. jealous
   f. frustrated
   g. impatient
   h. lonely
   i. sympathetic
   j. ashamed
   k. embarrassed
   l. surprised
   m. disappointed
   n. proud
   o. worried
   p. relieved

2. A child in your class made you feel:
   a. happy
   b. angry
   c. sad
   d. afraid
   e. jealous
   f. frustrated
   g. impatient
   h. lonely
   i. sympathetic
   j. ashamed
   k. embarrassed
   l. surprised
   m. disappointed
   n. proud
   o. worried
   p. relieved

3. You learned something you didn't know about a child through ICPS dialoguing.

4. When a child or children were having a problem, you thought you knew what the problem was, but because you used dialoguing you found out it was actually something quite different.

You can also use the ICPS Teacher Self-Evaluation Checklist, which immediately follows, to help you evaluate your ability to apply ICPS principles in various interpersonal situations. Duplicate the checklist and monitor your use of the ICPS approach either daily or weekly. Over time, average your score within each category as you use the checklist. As your score decreases for Categories A through C, and increases for Category D, you are increasing your use of the ICPS approach.

# ICPS TEACHER SELF-EVALUATION CHECKLIST

Date(s) _____

Rating Scale:     1         2         3         4         5
              Never                   Sometimes            Always

(Today/this week) I found that with most children, I:

### A. Demanded, commanded, belittled, punished

Score _____

*Examples*    Sit down!
           You can't do that!
           You know you shouldn't _____!
           How many times have I told you _____!
           Give it back!

### B. Offered suggestions without explanation

Score _____

*Examples*    You can't go around hitting kids.
           Why don't you ask him for it?
           Children must learn to share.

### C. Offered suggestions with explanation, including talk of feelings

Score _____

*Examples*    If you hit, you might lose a friend (get hurt).
           If you grab, she won't let you play with her toys.
           You shouldn't do that. It's not nice (fair).
           You'll make him ANGRY if you do that.

### D. Guided children to think of feelings, solutions, consequences

Score _____

*Examples*    What's the problem? What happened?
           How do you think (I/someone else) feel(s)
           when _____?
           What happened (MIGHT happen if) _____ ?
           What could you do so that would NOT happen?
           Do you think that IS or is NOT a good idea?
           *(If not a good idea:* Can you think of
           a DIFFERENT way to _____ ?)

# APPENDIX B

# ICPS Dialoguing Reminders

Post the following pages in your classroom to help remind yourself and other teachers to use ICPS dialoguing when real problems arise during the day. As the dialogues in the lessons suggest, it is important to be flexible. The steps presented here are meant to serve only as a guideline.

Happy ICPSing!

# CHILD-CHILD PROBLEMS

**STEP 1:**     **Define the problem.**

What happened? What's the matter?
That will help me understand the problem better.

**STEP 2:**     **Elicit feelings.**

How do you feel?
How does _____ feel?

**STEP 3:**     **Elicit consequences.**

What happened when you did that?

**STEP 4:**     **Elicit feelings about consequences.**

How did you feel when _____?
(*For example:* He took your pencil/she hit you)

**STEP 5:**     **Encourage the child to think of alternative solutions.**

Can you think of a DIFFERENT way to solve this problem so _____?
(*For example:* You both won't be mad/she won't hit you)

**STEP 6:**     **Encourage evaluation of the solution.**

Is that a good idea or not a good idea?
*If a good idea:* Go ahead and try that.
*If not a good idea:* Oh, you'll have to think of something DIFFERENT.

**STEP 7:**     **Encourage the child to think of potential obstacles.**

Could anything stop you from doing that?

**STEP 8:**     **Encourage sequential thinking.**

What is the next thing you could say or do?

**STEP 9:**     **Guide thought about time or timing.**

How long might that take?
Is this a GOOD TIME to do that?

**STEP 10:**     **Praise the child's act of thinking.**

You're thinking this through very well.

# TEACHER-CHILD PROBLEMS

**Can I talk to you and to _____ at the SAME TIME?**


**Is that a GOOD PLACE to _____?**

(*For example:* Draw/leave your food)

**Can you think of a GOOD PLACE to _____?**


**Is this a GOOD TIME to _____?**

(*For example:* Talk to your neighbor/talk to me)

**When is a GOOD TIME?**


**How do you think I feel when you _____?**

(*For example:* Don't listen/throw food/interrupt me)


**Can you think of something DIFFERENT to do until _____?**

(*For example:* I can get what you want/I can help you)